EYEWITNESS
CRYSTAL
& GEM

Apatite

Cut topazes

Danburite

Chalcedony

Opal

Calcite

Sphaerocobaltite

EYEWITNESS
CRYSTAL
& GEM

Written by
Dr. R. F. SYMES and Dr. R. R. HARDING

Crocoite

Dumortierite
bottle

Cut garnets

Cut tourmalines

Aragonite

Microcline

Meta-tobernite

DK

Malachite

Gold

Cut tourmaline

Cut topaz

Cut sapphire

Mother of pearl

Crocoite

DK

LONDON, NEW YORK,
MELBOURNE, MUNICH, AND DELHI

Project editor Louise Pritchard
Art editor Thomas Keenes
Senior editor Helen Parker
Senior art editors Julia Harris, Jacquie Gulliver
Production Louise Barrat
Picture research Cynthia Hole
Special photography Colin Keates ABIPP (Natural History Museum, London)

RELAUNCH EDITION (DK UK)
Editor Ashwin Khurana
US editor Margaret Parrish
Senior designers Rachael Grady, Spencer Holbrook
Managing editor Gareth Jones
Managing art editor Philip Letsu
Publisher Andrew Macintyre
Producer, preproduction Adam Stoneham
Senior producer Charlotte Cade
Jacket editor Maud Whatley
Jacket designer Laura Brim
Jacket design development manager Sophia MTT
Publishing director Jonathan Metcalf
Associate publishing director Liz Wheeler
Art director Phil Ormerod

RELAUNCH EDITION (DK INDIA)
Editors Surbhi Nayyar Kapoor, Priyanka Kharbanda
Art editors Deep Shikha Walia, Vikas Chauhan
Senior DTP designer Harish Aggarwal
DTP designers Anita Yadav, Pawan Kumar
Managing editor Alka Thakur Hazarika
Managing art editor Romi Chakraborty
CTS manager Balwant Singh
Jacket editorial manager Saloni Talwar
Jacker designers Govind Mittal, Suhita Dharamjit, Vidit Vashisht

First American Edition, 1991
This American Edition, 2014
Published in the United States by DK Publishing
4th floor, 345 Hudson Street
New York, New York 10014

14 15 16 17 18 10 9 8 7 6 5 4 3 2
196450—07/14

A catalog record for this book is available from the Library of Congress.

ISBN 978-1-4654-2052-7 (Paperback)
ISBN 978-1-4654-2093-0 (ALB)

DK books are available at special discounts when purchased in bulk for sales promotions, premiums, fund-raising, or educational use. For details, contact: DK Publishing Special Markets, 345 Hudson Street, New York, New York 10014 or SpecialSale@dk.com.

Color reproduction by Alta Image Ltd., London, UK
Printed and bound by South China Printing Co. Ltd., China

Discover more at

www.dk.com

Tourmaline

Agate

Agate

Contents

Amethyst

What is a crystal?

Associated with perfection, transparency, and clarity (although most are not perfect or transparent), crystals are solid materials with atoms in regular patterns (pp. 14–15). Many substances "crystallize," or grow in specific geometric forms with smooth plane surfaces. "Crystal" comes from the Greek word *kryos*, meaning icy—in ancient times, rock crystal was thought to be frozen so hard it would never melt.

States of matter

A material, such as water, can exist as a solid, liquid, or gas, depending on its temperature. In water vapor, or steam, molecules move around vigorously; in liquid they move slowly; in solid (ice) they form a regular order as a crystalline solid.

Familiar faces

These crystals, formed from hot solutions within the Earth, show characteristic faces (plane surfaces).

Tourmaline crystal

Quartz crystal

Albite crystals

Crystal minority

Most crystals in this book are of natural, solid, inorganic materials called minerals. Some inorganic compounds also form crystals; this potassium magnesium sulfate is an artificially grown crystal.

Massive mineral

Crystals will grow large and perfect in the right conditions. Most grow irregularly (called massive), such as this specimen of the mineral scapolite with small, poorly formed crystals.

Glass house

London's Crystal Palace (built 1851) had nearly 300,000 panes of glass—not crystals—as its roof and outer walls.

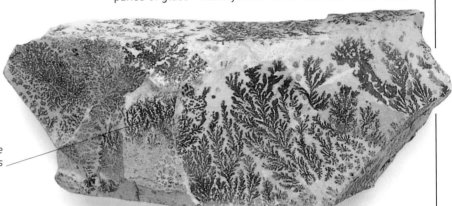

Pyrolusite dendrites

18th-century painting of an Indian woman bedecked with jewelry

Cut heliodor (pp. 38–39)

Gem of a crystal

Most gemstones are natural crystals chosen for their beauty, durability, and rarity. They are usually cut and polished (pp. 58–59). Crystals can now also be grown artificially (pp. 26–27) and cut as gemstones.

Cut aquamarine (pp. 38–39)

Crystal lining

These fernlike growths, or dentrites (p. 21), often found lining rock cracks, look like a plant but are crystalline growths of the mineral pyrolusite.

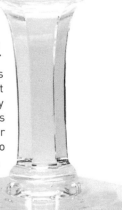

Most irregular

Some of the objects we call "crystal" are glass. Glass has little structure, as it is cooled too quickly for the atoms to form a regular order. It is said to be amorphous.

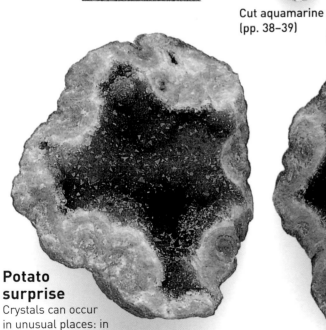

Potato surprise

Crystals can occur in unusual places: in plowed fields of south England, irregular nodules known as "potato stones" have sparkling crystals inside.

A world of crystals

Crystals are all around us. The rocks that form the Earth, the Moon, and meteorites (pieces of rock from space) are made up of minerals, most of which are formed of crystals. Minerals are crystalline solids composed of atoms of various elements. The most important elements are oxygen, silicon, and six metallic elements including iron and calcium. We use crystals at home (pp. 62–63), work (pp. 28–29), and in technology.

Crystal layers
The Earth has three layers—core, mantle, and crust—made mostly of solid, rock-forming minerals. Some rocks are formed of one mineral; most are made of two or more.

Orthoclase

Quartz

Biotite

Granite
Granite is the most characteristic rock of Earth's continental crust (outer layer), made mainly of the minerals quartz, feldspar, and mica. Here, large crystals of the feldspar mineral orthoclase can be seen.

Eclogite
The Earth's upper mantle is likely mostly peridotite, with other crystals such as eclogite. This rock is eclogite with green pyroxene and small garnets in it.

Garnet crystal

Meteorite
The center (core) of the Earth may be similarly composed to this iron meteorite. It has been treated to reveal its crystalline structure.

Liquid rock
Molten lava can erupt from volcanoes such as Kilauea, Hawaii, shown here. When lava cools, minerals crystallize into solid rock.

Strength
Most buildings are made of crystals: rocky materials are mostly crystalline, and the strength of cement depends on crystals growing.

Down to dust

Pebbles, sand, and soil parts are all formed from eroded rocks and will finally be eroded to dust (p. 32). All these things are made of crystals.

Feldspar crystal

Basalt pebble

Quartzite pebbles

Quartz sand grains

Soil

Crystal cave

Fine stalactites and stalagmites form the spectacular scenery in these grottos in Lebanon.

Drip by drip

Mostly made of calcite crystals, these stalagmites grew in an old mine as water, rich in calcium carbonate, dripped down.

Calcite crystals

Live crystals

The elements that make up most rock-forming minerals are also important to life on Earth. For example, minerals such as calcite and apatite crystallize inside plants and animals.

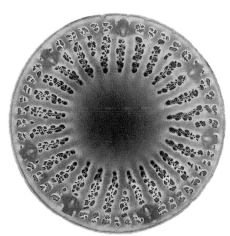

Microcrystals

This microscope diatom, *Cyclotella pseudostelligera*, is algae. Its cell walls are made up of tiny silica crystals.

Animal mineral

This gallstone from a cow's bladder has the same crystalline composition as struvite, a naturally occurring mineral.

Stressful

This greatly enlarged picture of epinephrine— a hormone produced by the body— shows it is crystalline.

Human apatite

Bones, such as this human humerus (upper arm bone), contain tiny crystals of the mineral apatite.

Natural beauty

Well-formed crystals are beautiful and rare. Conditions have to be perfect for them to grow (pp. 20–21) and survive, and any changes in conditions must protect, not destroy, them. The crystals shown are 60 percent their real size.

Proustite
These cherry-red crystals are known as ruby silvers, and are often found with silver deposits. These are from the silver mine area Chanarcillo, Copiapo, Chile, worked between 1830 and 1880.

Bournonite
These bright-gray "cog-wheel" crystals are from the Herodsfoot lead mine, near Liskeard in Cornwall, England. This mine produced quality bournonite crystals from 1850 to 1875.

Crystal Dream, a science fiction creation based on crystal shapes by French artist Jean "Moebius" Giraud

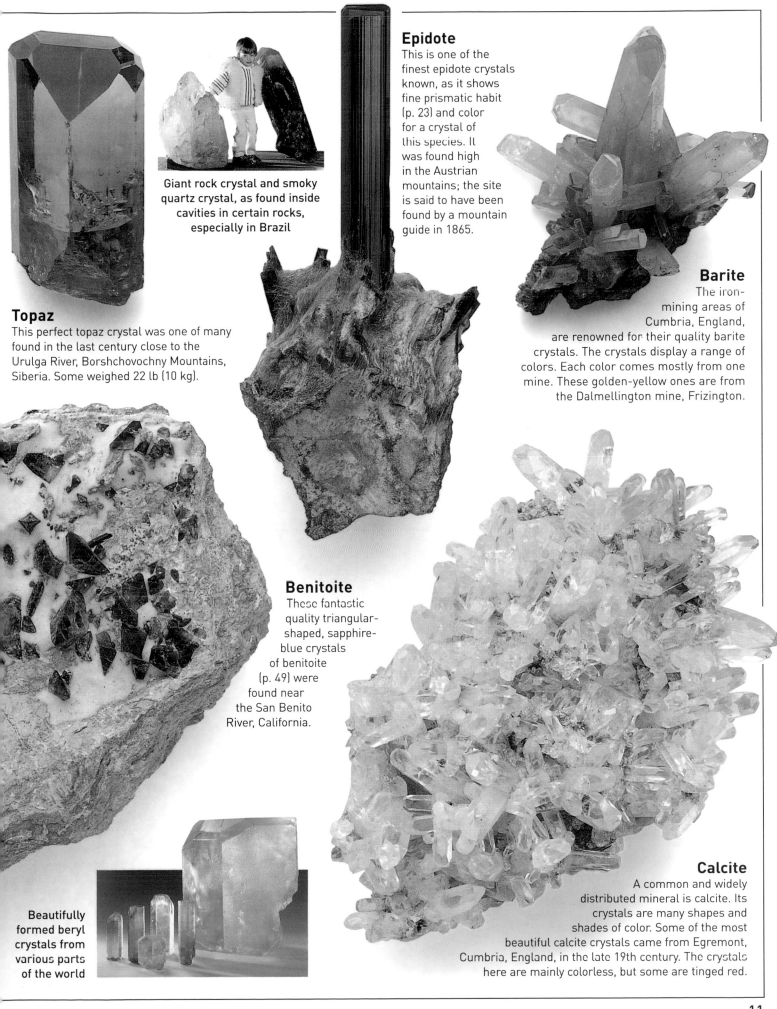

Epidote
This is one of the finest epidote crystals known, as it shows fine prismatic habit (p. 23) and color for a crystal of this species. It was found high in the Austrian mountains; the site is said to have been found by a mountain guide in 1865.

Giant rock crystal and smoky quartz crystal, as found inside cavities in certain rocks, especially in Brazil

Topaz
This perfect topaz crystal was one of many found in the last century close to the Urulga River, Borshchovochny Mountains, Siberia. Some weighed 22 lb (10 kg).

Barite
The iron-mining areas of Cumbria, England, are renowned for their quality barite crystals. The crystals display a range of colors. Each color comes mostly from one mine. These golden-yellow ones are from the Dalmellington mine, Frizington.

Benitoite
These fantastic quality triangular-shaped, sapphire-blue crystals of benitoite (p. 49) were found near the San Benito River, California.

Beautifully formed beryl crystals from various parts of the world

Calcite
A common and widely distributed mineral is calcite. Its crystals are many shapes and shades of color. Some of the most beautiful calcite crystals came from Egremont, Cumbria, England, in the late 19th century. The crystals here are mainly colorless, but some are tinged red.

11

On the surface

A well-formed crystal has symmetrical (regular) features, such as faces with parallel edges. Crystals may have three types of symmetry: "plane of symmetry" is the imaginary line separating two sides that mirror each other; "axis of symmetry" is the imaginary line about which a crystal is rotated and shows the same pattern of faces multiple times—if the pattern appears twice it is twofold, if three, threefold; and a crystal with "center of symmetry" is edged by pairs of parallel faces.

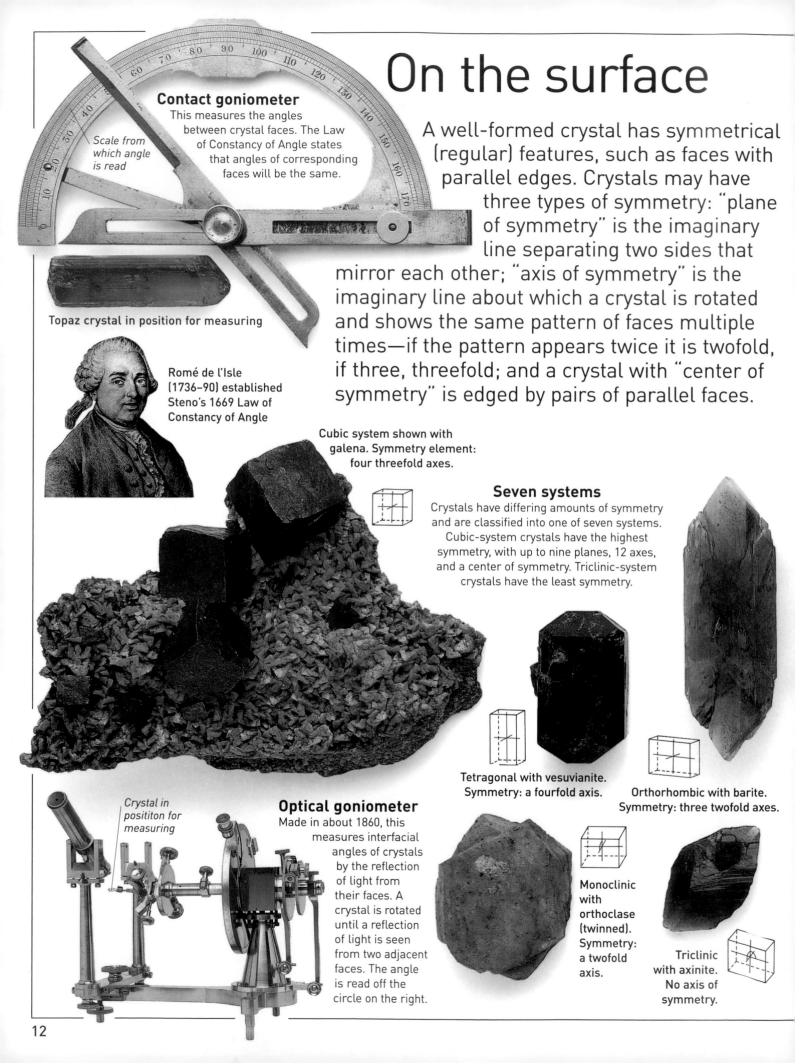

Contact goniometer
This measures the angles between crystal faces. The Law of Constancy of Angle states that angles of corresponding faces will be the same.

Scale from which angle is read

Topaz crystal in position for measuring

Romé de l'Isle (1736–90) established Steno's 1669 Law of Constancy of Angle

Cubic system shown with galena. Symmetry element: four threefold axes.

Seven systems
Crystals have differing amounts of symmetry and are classified into one of seven systems. Cubic-system crystals have the highest symmetry, with up to nine planes, 12 axes, and a center of symmetry. Triclinic-system crystals have the least symmetry.

Tetragonal with vesuvianite. Symmetry: a fourfold axis.

Orthorhombic with barite. Symmetry: three twofold axes.

Crystal in position for measuring

Optical goniometer
Made in about 1860, this measures interfacial angles of crystals by the reflection of light from their faces. A crystal is rotated until a reflection of light is seen from two adjacent faces. The angle is read off the circle on the right.

Monoclinic with orthoclase (twinned). Symmetry: a twofold axis.

Triclinic with axinite. No axis of symmetry.

Same but different

Some crystallographers (studiers of crystals) think the trigonal system is part of the hexagonal. Both have the same set of axes but the trigonal has threefold symmetry.

Symmetry design

This repetitive maple-leaf design is based on crystal symmetry. It was a made for a Union of Crystallography meet, held in Canada in 1981.

Trigonal with calcite. Symmetry: a threefold axis.

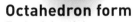

Hexagonal with beryl. Symmetry: a sixfold axis.

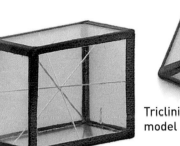

Triclinic model

Cubic model

Crystal models

These help crystallographers with symmetry. The cotton threads between the faces show axes of rotation.

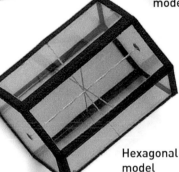

Hexagonal model

Form

Crystals of the same mineral may not look alike. The same faces on two crystals may be different sizes and so form different-shaped crystals. Crystals may also vary in "form." Shown here are three forms found in the cubic crystal system, illustrated with pyrite.

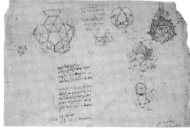

Leonardo da Vinci's studies of the transformation of geometrical bodies

Cube form

Each of the six square faces of 90° angles intersect one of the fourfold axes, and is parallel to the other two.

Octahedron form

Each of the eight equilateral triangular faces intersects three of the fourfold axes.

Pyritohedron

This form (also, pentagonal dodecahedron) has 12 five-sided faces.

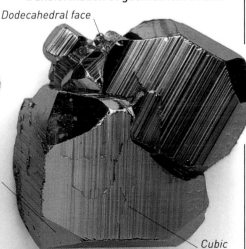

Dodecahedral face

Octahedral face

Cubic face

Diagram to show the relationship between different cubic forms

Octahedron

Cube and octahedron

Cube

Cube and pyritohedron

Pyritohedron

Combination of forms

Cubic faces combine with octahedral faces and poorly developed dodecahedral faces.

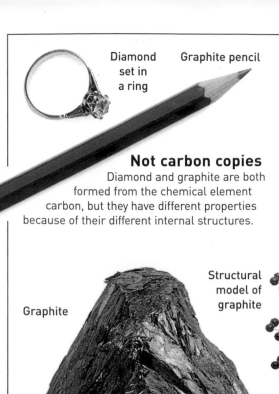

Diamond set in a ring

Graphite pencil

Inside crystals

A crystal's properties, such as regular shape, are decided by its internal structure of atoms. Each atom has a set place, tied to others by bonds. The atoms of a mineral always group the same way to form its crystals. One of the first to see an inner regularity was Abbé Hauy, in 1784. With X-ray discovery in 1895, von Laue realized X-rays could be used to see atomic structure.

Not carbon copies
Diamond and graphite are both formed from the chemical element carbon, but they have different properties because of their different internal structures.

Graphite

Structural model of graphite

Graphite
Graphite's carbon atoms are linked in a hexagonal way in widely spaced layers. These weak bonds make it a soft mineral.

Diamond crystal

Diamond
Each carbon atom is strongly bonded to four others. This makes diamond very hard.

Structural model of diamond

Augite crystal

Actinolite
Silicate minerals, in all common rocks except limestone, have a tetrahedron makeup: one silicon and four oxygen atoms (SiO_4). Actinolite's structure is based on a double chain of tetrahedra.

Gold atoms
This photograph shows the atomic lattice of gold magnified millions of times. Each yellow blob is an atom.

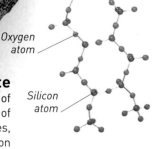

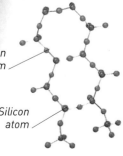

Oxygen atom

Augite
Augite is one of an important group of silicates, the pyroxenes, with a structure based on one chain of SiO_4 tetrahedra.

Silicon atom

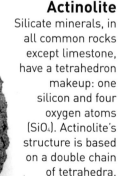

Model showing SiO_4 tetrahedra in a single-chain silicate

Tetrahedra double chain

Beryl

Beryl (pp. 38–39) and other silicate minerals' internal structure has groups of six tetrahedra, linked in rings.

Max von Laue

In 1912, with X-ray photos, von Laue showed atoms in crystals.

Wavelength (meters)	
	Gamma rays
10^{-15}	
10^{-11}	
10^{-9}	X-rays
10^{-7}	Ultraviolet radiation
10^{-6}	Visible light
10^{-4}	Infrared radiation (heat)
	Microwaves
1	
	Radio waves
10^{6}	

Decreasing wavelength

Electromagnetic waves

X-rays are part of the electromagnetic radiation spectrum. All radiations can be described in terms of waves, such as light, radio, and heat. The waves differ in length and frequency. White light, visible to the human eye, is electromagnetic waves varying in length between red and violet in the spectrum (p. 16).

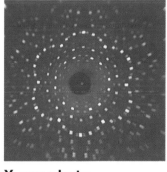

X-ray photo

This von Laue photo shows the symmetrical pattern in beryl, related to the hexagonal symmetry of the crystal.

Cleavage

Some crystals split along planes called cleavage planes, which are the same for all crystals of a species. They form along the structure's weakest planes and are proof of the orderly line-up of atoms.

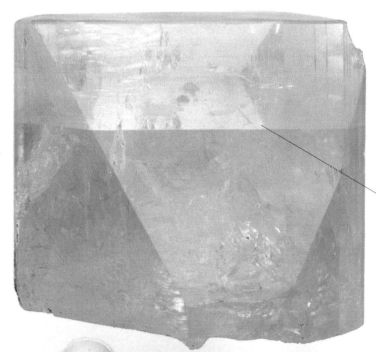

Topaz

This blue topaz crystal from Madagascar has a perfect cleavage. Topaz has isolated SiO₄ groups in its structure.

Cleavage plane

Micas

In this group of silicates, the atom bonds at 90° to its "sheet structure" are weak. Cleavage occurs easily along these planes.

Thin cleavage flakes

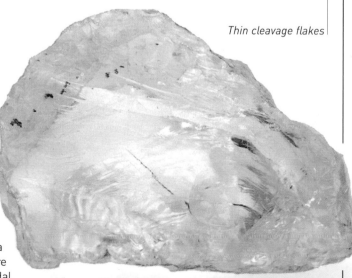

Abbé Hauy

Hauy saw how calcite regularly fractures into rhombs along cleavage planes, and he realized a crystal's regular shape was because of an inner regularity.

Quartz

Quartz structure is based on a strongly bonded network of silicon and oxygen atoms. Crystals do not split easily but show a smooth, curved fracture known as conchoidal.

Moonstones
These (p. 45) have a white or blue sheen from layers of tiny albite crystals within orthoclase.

Crystal color

Crystal color can be striking. Something looks a specific color as your eye and brain react to light wavelengths (p. 15). When white light (daylight) falls on a crystal, some wavelengths may be reflected, some absorbed. If some are absorbed, you see a color other than white because some white light wavelengths are missing.

Transparent, colorless rock crystal

Transparent, purple amethyst

Opaque milky quartz

Transparent or opaque
Crystals can be transparent (see through, letting nearly all light through), translucent (letting some light through), or opaque (are not see through, letting no light through).

Idiochromatic

Some minerals are nearly always the same color because certain light-absorbing atoms are an essential part of their crystal structure. These minerals are described as idiochromatic.

Isaac Newton (1642–1727)
Sir Isaac Newton was a famous English scientist who discovered that white light can be separated into seven colors. He explained it with a theory of the rainbow.

A spectrum, from dispersion of white light in a prism

Sulfur
This idiochromatic mineral normally crystallizes in bright yellow crystals, often found near volcanic vents (p. 20).

Azurite
This copper mineral is always blue—hence the term azure blue. It was used as a pigment in ancient times.

Allochromatic

Some minerals are allochromatic—they are a range of colors due to impurities or light-absorbing defects in the atomic structure. For example, quartz and diamond can be red, green, yellow, and blue.

Rhodochrosite
Manganese minerals such as this are usually pink or red. Some beryls are bright red due to small amounts of manganese.

Erythrite
Cobalt minerals are usually pink or reddish. Trace amounts of cobalt may color colorless minerals.

Fluorite
Some minerals are fluorescent—they are various colors in ultraviolet (UV) light (p. 15). This is usually caused by foreign atoms (activators) in the crystal structure. This fluorite crystal is blue in UV light, but green in daylight.

Play of colors

Some minerals have a play of colors, like that in an oil film or soap bubble. This may be produced when the light is affected by the physical structure of the crystals, such as twinning (p. 21), cleavage planes (p. 15), or by the development during growth of thin films. Microscopic intergrowths of platelike inclusions (p. 21) also cause light interference.

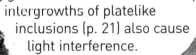

Salt
A missing atom in a crystal's structure can form a color center. Coloration of common salt is thought to be caused by this.

Hematite
The play of colors on these crystals is called iridescence. It is due to the interference of light in thin surface films.

Labradorite
This feldspar mineral often forms dull gray crystalline masses. Internal twinning causes interference of light, which gives the mineral a sheen, or schiller, with patches of different colors.

Identification

To identify a crystal, its properties must be tested. Color (pp. 16–17), habit (pp. 22–23), cleavage (p. 15), and surface features are physical properties that can be studied using a hand lens. Others, such as hardness and specific gravity (SG), require basic equipment. Sophisticated instruments are needed to test for atomic structure and chemical composition.

The fictitious Sherlock Holmes was a master of investigation and identification

Identity crisis
These gemstones are the same color, but are different minerals: topaz (left) and citrine (right).

Seeing double
Birefringence, or double refraction, occurs in some crystals. In this rhomb of calcite, light is split into two rays, causing a doubled image.

Doubled image of yarn seen through calcite

Chemical beam balance being used to determine specific gravity

Orthoclase SG = 2.6

Galena SG = 7.4

Specific gravity
An important property, SG is the ratio of a substance's weight compared to that of an equal volume of water. These crystals are similar in size but their SG is different, reflecting how the atoms are packed together.

Hardness

The property of hardness depends on the strength of the forces holding a solid's atoms together. In 1812, F. Mohs devised a scale of hardness, using 10 minerals. Each can scratch only those below it on the scale. Intervals of hardness are roughly equal except for between corundum (9) and diamond (10).

1
Talc

2
Gypsum

3
Calcite

4
Fluorite

Probing around

Electron probe microanalysis was used to investigate the specimen (left). In a scanning electron microscope (SEM), a beam of electrons was focused on the specimen, producing an X-ray spectrum (below).

10
Diamond

The X-ray spectrum showing large peaks for iron (Fe), arsenic (As), calcium (Ca), and zinc (Zn)

Mistaken identity

Modern techniques can better reveal chemical composition. X-ray showed these small, blue-gray crystals on limonite to be the mineral symplesite (hydrated iron arsenate). But further analysis showed some unexpected calcium and zinc, too.

Ruby, colored by chromium

Almandine garnet, by iron

Absorbed in stone

A spectroscope can distinguish between similarly colored gems. It shows dark bands on the spectrum (p. 16) where wavelengths have been absorbed by the gem.

Shadow play

Refractive index (RI) measures, using a refractometer, how well a mineral bends light. It is useful in identification. The position of the shadow from light passing through the stone gives the RI.

Spinel RI: 1.71

Tourmaline RI: 1.62 and 1.64

9
Corundum

Diamond

8
Topaz

Sapphire

7
Quartz

Chrysoberyl

Topaz

6
Orthoclase

5
Apatite

Opal

Peridot

Garnet

Amethyst

Friedrich Mohs

Mohs (1773–1839) was a professor of mineralogy in Graz, Austria, when he developed the hardness scale.

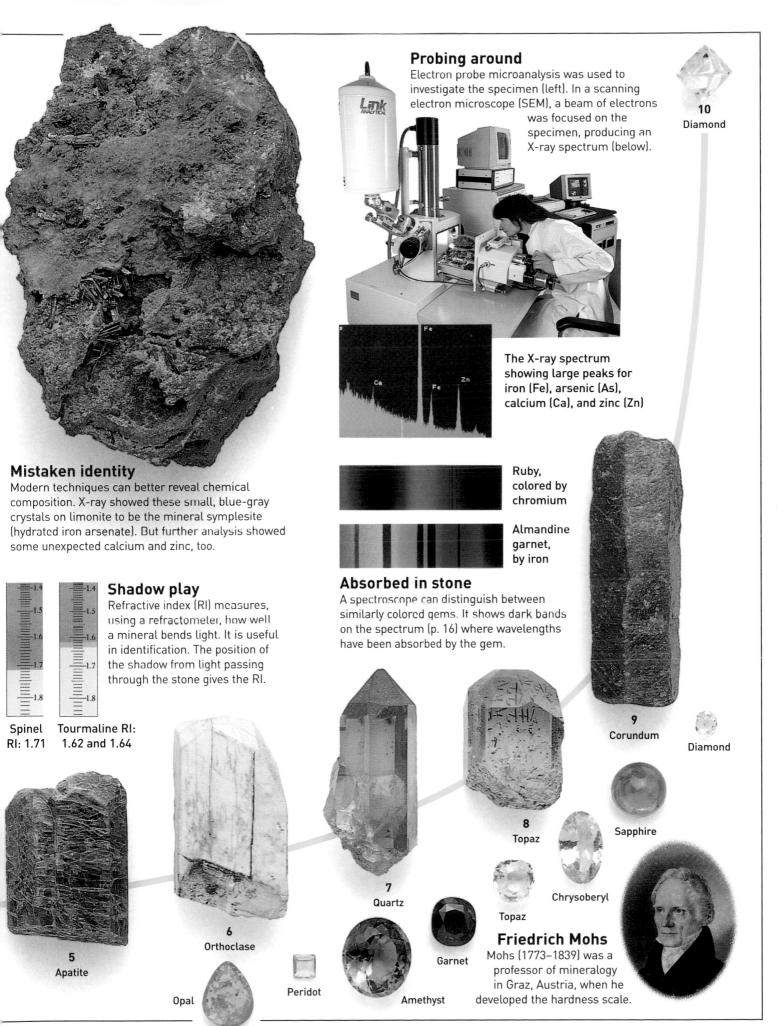

19

Natural growth

Crystals grow as atoms arrange themselves in a regular network (pp. 14–15), layer by layer. Growth continues by adding material to the outer surfaces. Temperature, pressure, chemical conditions, and space all affect growth. In an hour, millions of atoms arrange themselves across a crystal face. It is not surprising then that defects occur—a perfect crystal is rare.

Crystal layers
This photomicrograph (magnified image) shows the layers of different crystals in a thin section of magmatic rock.

Twisted
Crystals can be bent, like this stibnite, perhaps caused by mechanical bending as they grow.

Mineral springs
Hot, watery solutions and gases containing minerals, such as sal ammoniac, reach the Earth's surface in hot springs or gas vents. Here, the minerals may crystallize.

Sal ammoniac crystals

In the pocket
Crystals may grow in rock cavities. This gem pocket (a cavity with gem-quality crystals) at Mt. Mica, Maine, was discovered in 1979.

Settling down
As magma cools, crystals of various minerals form. Some build up in layers, as different minerals crystallize at varying times.

Changed by force
These blue kyanite and brown staurolite crystals were formed by metamorphism: high temperatures and pressures in the Earth's crust caused minerals to recrystallize, forming new minerals.

Siderite

Quartz

Chalcopyrite

Taking shape
Many minerals crystallize from watery solutions. The crystals can reveal the sequence of events. Here, a fluorite crystal grew, was coated with siderite, but then dissolved. The siderite coating kept fluorite's cubic shape. Finally, quartz and chalcopyrite crystals grew in the cube.

Building blocks
Skyscrapers are built like crystals—by adding layers to the same symmetrical shape.

Etch pit

Beryl etching
Solutions or hot gases may dissolve crystal surfaces (above), forming regularly shaped hollows, or etch pits. Their shape reflects atomic structure.

Spiraling round
Crystal faces are rarely flat, due to growth defects. This magnified image shows that atoms form a continuous spiral instead of layers across the crystal face.

Twinning
During crystallization, two crystals of the same mineral may develop to be joined at a common plane. These are known as twinned crystals. The imaginary line between the two parts is the twin plane.

Butterfly twins
This calcite shows a butterfly contact twin crystal, named after its likeness to butterfly wings.

Growing up together
When the two parts of twin crystals are intergrown, they are called penetration twins.

Form competition
Many crystals have parallel lines, or striations, on their faces. These can be caused by two forms (p. 13) trying to grow at the same time.

Striations on pyrite crystal

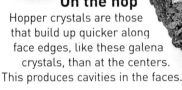

On the hop
Hopper crystals are those that build up quicker along face edges, like these galena crystals, than at the centers. This produces cavities in the faces.

Crystal enclosure
During growth, a crystal may enclose crystals of other minerals. These are known as inclusions.

Fluid inclusion

Rutile inclusions in quartz

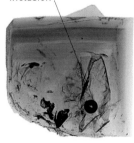

Phantom quartz
Interruptions in a crystal's growth can produce regular inclusions. Parallel growth layers ("phantoms"), as in this quartz, formed as dark-green chlorite coated the crystal during growth breaks.

"Phantom" growth layers

Fluorite crystal with inclusions

Good habits

A crystal's shape is called its habit. It is important in crystallography and is very useful in identification. The forms (p. 13) or group of forms that a crystal develops are often what give it a particular habit. As crystals grow, some faces develop more than others and their relative sizes create different shapes. Most minerals occur in groups and rarely show fine crystal shapes. These are aggregates.

Tabular
This large red crystal of wulfenite is from the Red Cloud mine in Arizona. Its habit is tabular. Such crystals can be extremely thin.

Two forms
The calcite crystal "mushrooms" above show two forms: a scalenohedron forms the "stem" topped by a rhombohedra.

Stalactitic
These aggregates of goethite are stalactitic. Goethite is an important iron ore. This group is from Coblenz, Rhineland, Germany.

Massive
Crystals that grow in a mass, where individual crystals cannot be clearly seen, are called massive. Dumortierite is a rare mineral. It is usually massive, like this piece from Bahia, Brazil.

Acicular
The radiating, slender mesolite crystals in this aggregate are acicular (needlelike). They are very fragile and can pierce skin. This group is from Bombay, India.

Giant's Causeway
This formation in County Antrim, Northern Ireland, looks like hexagonal crystals but it jointed from contraction as basalt lava cooled.

Pisolitic
This polished limestone from the Czech Republic is pisolitic—it has small, round aggregates of concentric crystal layers.

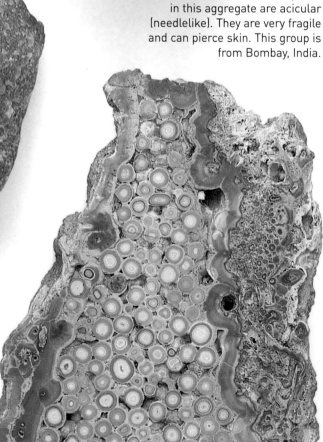

Dendritic

Dentritic, meaning treelike, describes the habit of these copper crystals from Broken Hill, New South Wales, Australia. Copper often forms in hydrothermal deposits, but is also found as grains in sandstones.

Prismatic

Beryl crystals are found in granite pegmatites (p. 25) and can grow to be large. These are from a quarry in Maine. More than 30 ft (9 m) long, they are prismatic—longer in one direction than the other.

Lenticular

Twinned (p. 21), clear crystals of gypsum form the "ears" on this mass of lenticular (lens-shaped) crystals from Winnipeg, Canada.

Twinned gypsum crystal

Bladed hornblende crystal

Globular calcite crystal aggregate

Coralloidal

Aggregated, coral-like crystals have a coralloidal habit. This mass of aragonite crystals is from Eisenberg, Styria, Austria.

Globular

These aggregated calcite crystals are globular (spherical). The others are clear quartz. This group came from Valenciana mine, Guanajuato, Mexico.

Bladed

This prismatic black crystal is a hornblende, the white crystals are analcime, and the others are prismatic serandite. The group was found at Mont St. Hilaire, Quebec, Canada.

Quartz in a cave

Physical and chemical conditions influence crystal growth. Many crystals grow in cavities, which can be huge caves, shown in this impression of a quartz grotto.

Extraction

The search for mineral deposits has taken place since prehistoric times. Some, such as copper, occur in great quantity; others like gold and diamond occur in smaller quantities but get higher prices. Profitable mining requires large quantities in one area and easy extraction by quarrying, panning and dredging, or deep mining. Minerals from which useful metals are extracted are called ores.

Miners descending the shaft at Wieliczka salt mine, Poland

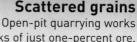
Chalcopyrite

Scattered grains
Open-pit quarrying works rocks of just one-percent ore. The ore, like this chalcopyrite copper ore, occurs as small grains, but the whole rock has to be worked. A huge hole and lots of gangue (waste) are produced.

Copper ore

Quartz

Rich vein
Larger amounts of ore occur in veins, but most high-grade ores have been found and worked out by deep mining. This vein has quartz and chalcopyrite in altered granite.

Romans in Cornwall
The Romans mined tin deposits in Cornwall, England. Mining techniques have improved, but ore is still crushed, isolated from gangue, and refined.

Ingot of refined Cornish tin, produced in 1860

Liroconite crystals from a secondary-enriched layer

Vein of covellite, a copper sulfide, from a secondary sulfide enrichment layer

Gradual improvement
Groundwaters filter down through rock and carry elements downward, redepositing them in a rock's lower layers. This secondary alteration and enrichment naturally improves low-grade ores to higher concentrations. These enriched layers in copper deposits may contain azurite and liroconite, or sulfide minerals, such as bornite and chalcocite.

Swirling waters
Panning is a simple way of separating minerals, often used to sort gem-rich river gravels in areas such as Myanmar. Swirling water in a pan washes away light gangue minerals, leaving wanted minerals behind.

Panning for gold in the Irrawaddy River, Myanmar

Last to go
Granite pegmatites tend to consist of large crystals and are the source of many fine gems, formed by the crystallization of the last fluids left after most of the granite has solidified.

Tourmaline crystal

Down under
Much mining takes place underground, as at the Coober Pedy opal mine in South Australia.

Smaller than some
These beryl crystals measure about 8 x 5½ in (20 x 14 cm), but are small compared to some crystals in pegmatites.

On the surface
The Argyle quarry in Western Australia is the world-leading diamond producer.

Growing crystals

Scientists have manufactured crystals for more than a century. Naturally grown crystals are flawed (pp. 20–21); synthetic ones can be made flawless and grown to a specific shape and size. Artificial crystals are vital to modern technology. Grown crystals are used in almost every electronic or optical device. It could be said that future developments in electronics depend on the development of crystal-growing techniques.

Meltdown
Artificial crystals like this bismuth are produced by melting and cooling metal. Bismuth is used in electric fuses.

In flux
Many emeralds are produced by flux fusion: a powder of emerald parts is heated with a flux (solid). The flux melts and powder dissolves. It is then left to cool and forms crystals over several months.

Cut synthetic emerald

Synthetic emerald crystal

Beyond Earth
An important science, this protein-crystal-growth experiment was on board the space shuttle *Discovery* with astronaut George Nelson in 1988.

Drawn out
Pure silicon does not occur naturally, so crystals are made. Quartz sand heated with coke produces nearly pure silicon. In one process, a seed crystal on a rotating rod is dipped into the melt and slowly removed, "drawing a crystal."

Melt technique

Excellent crystals may be grown by slow cooling or evaporation of a supersaturated solution (no more will dissolve) of a salt like ammonium dihydrogen phosphate (ADP). Here, powdered ADP with a chrome-alum impurity has dissolved in boiling water and cooled.

Liquid cools rapidly. Stubby but cloudy prismatic crystals form.

Crystals grow slowly, allowing them to become clearer.

At room temperature, crystals grow slowly due to evaporation.

Cooling stops, but evaporation continues. Crystals slowly grow.

Flame fusion

Flame fusion was perfected around 1900 by August Verneuil. Powdered material fed through a flame fuses into liquid and drips on a support. Pulling the support from the heat forms a crystal, or boule.

Henri Moisson (1852–1907)

Moisson tried to produce artificial diamonds in iron crucibles at the Edison workshops in Paris, France.

Eureka!

In 1970, the General Electric Company in the US announced the laboratory creation of gem-quality diamonds.

Support for growing crystal

Synthetic sapphire boule

Synthetic rubies produced in a crucible

Two halves of synthetic ruby boule

Grown in size

French chemist Fremy was the first to grow good-sized gem-quality crystals, in 1877. He made rubies by melting the materials and fusing them in a porcelain crucible at very high temperatures.

1890 crucible containing a mass of small gemstones

Abrasive character

The artificial material carborundum (silicon carbide) is produced in electrically fired furnaces with a charge of coke and sand. It is nearly as hard as diamond and is mostly used as an abrasive.

Hexagonal carborundum crystal

Gold fever

Over the years, many people have tried to find a way to change base metals into gold, as illustrated in *The Alchemist at Work* by David Teniers (1582–1649).

Crystals at work

Crystals play an important part in this age of rapid technological change. They are used in control circuits, machines, electronics, communications, industrial tools, medicine, and credit cards. New crystals for new purposes are always being developed. Crystal produced in the laboratory (pp. 26–27) include ruby laser rods, silicon chips, and diamonds for tools.

Diamond window
Because of their unique properties, diamonds have been used in space, where they have to withstand extreme conditions. Diamonds were part of an infrared radiometer experiment on the *Pioneer Venus* probe in which the temperature reached 840°F (450°C).

Silicon wafer

Silicon slice
Silicon chips are made from wafers (thin slices) cut from artificial crystals of pure silicon (p. 26). The wafers are etched with electronic circuits, which are transferred to the wafer from a matrix (piece of film).

Silicon chip matrix

Silicon chip in protective covering

Circuits
Many different chips are needed in a computer. Each chip has a different circuit to run a specific part. Every chip is protected in a case, then linked to others on a circuit board.

Smart cards
Every "smart card" contains a tiny mini computer on a silicon chip. When the card is inserted into a reading device, the chip connects with an electrical reader that scans the information on the card. Smart cards are used for driver's licenses, identity cards, and transit cards.

Location of silicon chip

Ruby rod
Synthetic ruby crystals are used to make a beam of pure red laser light. Their heated atoms are stimulated by light to emit radiation waves.

Lasers
Laser beams can be focused to tiny points generating intense heat, put to use in welding, drilling, and surgery.

Diamond tools

Diamonds are widely used for sawing, drilling, grinding, and polishing—from quarrying stone to delicate eye surgery—mainly because they are so hard. They come in a range of sizes, shapes, and strengths. More than 80 percent of industrial diamonds are synthetic.

A surgeon using a diamond-bladed scalpel in delicate eye surgery

Drill bits
Diamond-tipped drill bits are used on all types of rock and in many industries; for instance, diamond-tipped bits are used to drill oil wells. The diamonds are different shapes for different uses. Some drill bits contain surface diamonds; others use diamond grit.

Drill bit impregnated with synthetic diamond grit

Drill bit containing surface-set natural diamonds

Diamond scalpel
In addition to being hard, diamond does not corrode. This is one reason diamonds are used in surgery.

Diamond blade

Diamond grit
Grit and powders, used for polishing and grinding, are mainly made from synthetic diamonds.

Diamond wire
Cutting with a diamond wire reduces material loss. It can be used to cut stone from quarries and in demolition of concrete buildings. The wire can be used around a drum or as a continuous loop.

"Bead" containing synthetic diamond abrasive

Cutting segment containing synthetic diamond grit

Saw blade
Diamond-set saws are used for cutting glass and rocks. The blades have industrial diamonds in a "carrier" such as brass, bonded to a steel disk. The carrier wears away to expose new diamonds.

Cutting an opening for a window in brickwork using a diamond saw

Good vibrations

Brazil quartz mines
Brazil's quartz crystals were important for electronics before synthetic crystals were grown (pp. 26–27).

Quartz is a common mineral. It is widely found as veins (p. 24) and with other mineral deposits, and is a main constituent of granite, sandstones, and sand. As quartzite and sandstone, it is used for building and manufacturing glass. Its crystals have a piezoelectric effect, used to measure pressure and in gas lighters, and quartz crystal oscillators provide stable frequency control in televisions.

Quartz

Waves of energy
Quartz crystals are used in electronics. They can change a mechanical force, such as a blow from a hammer, into electrical energy.

English prism
Quartz commonly crystallizes as six-sided prisms with rhombohedral ends (pp. 12–13). The prism axis shows only threefold symmetry. On many crystals, alternate faces show different growth patterns.

Six-sided prismatic crystal

Crystal trio
Large crystals of quartz can be seen in this granite pegmatite crystal group (p. 25), along with fine crystals of feldspar and mica.

Mica   *Feldspar*

Gold

Quartz

Going for gold
Many quartz veins carry metallic mineral deposits (p. 24). This specimen, from the famous area of British gold extraction at St. David's mine, Gwynedd, Wales, contains gold. The quartz and gold were deposited by hydrothermal fluids. In mining, the quartz would be considered a gangue (unwanted mineral).

Small face showing left-handedness

Right-handed quartz crystal

Ambidextrous
In quartz crystals, silicon and oxygen atoms are joined in a tetrahedron (four-sided triangular pyramid). Linked in spirals, they can be left- or right-handed. This structure accounts for quartz piezoelectricity.

Left-handed quartz crystal

Crystal healing
In this ancient art, it is thought that as light reflects off crystals the electromagnetic field of the body (the aura) absorbs energy. The person is then aware of causes of physical disease, and heals.

Crystal clear
Crystals from groups, like this one from Arkansas, are prized for their beauty and clarity, and are often used in crystal healing.

Alpine architecture
This "twisted" group of smoky quartz crystals shows some beautiful crystal "architecture." Such crystal groups are often found in the Alps in Europe.

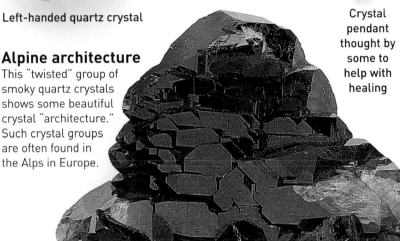

Crystal pendant thought by some to help with healing

Healing power
Because of its common crystal perfection, quartz is used in crystal healing. Here, stones and crystals have been placed on vital nerve points.

Piezoelectricity
In 1880, Pierre and Jacques Curie discovered that pressure on a quartz crystal causes positive and negative charges across it—piezoelectricity. It was later found that alternating electrical charges cause a piezoelectric crystal to vibrate—the basis for quartz use as oscillators to control radio waves, or keep time.

Jacques and Pierre Curie with their parents

Pure necessity
Synthetic crystals like this are grown by a hydrothermal process (p. 26) to make oscillator plates.

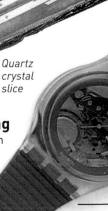

Watch piece
This micro-thin quartz crystal slice is used to keep time in a quartz watch.

Quartz crystal slice

Split-second timing
The crystal slice in a watch vibrates more than 30,000 times per second, making it a good timekeeper.

Quartz

Quartz is silicon dioxide. It occurs as crystals and fine-grained masses (called jaspers or chalcedonies) in many forms, patterns, and colors. In the right conditions, giant crystals can grow—the largest recorded was 20 ft (6 m) long and more than 53 tons (48 metric tons). Quartz is tough with no cleavage (p. 15), making it ideal for carving and cutting; it is widely used as a gem.

Quartz crystal
Crystal system: trigonal; hardness: 7; specific gravity: 2.65.

Dunes and dust
Quartz forms part of sand and dust, and so dust can damage gems of 6 or less on Mohs' hardness scale.

Single crystals

Single crystals of quartz include amethyst, rose and smoky quartz, colorless rock crystal, and yellow citrine. They're often big enough to be cut as gems.

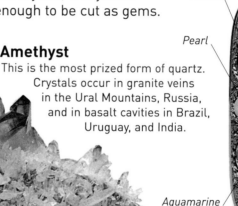

Amethyst
This is the most prized form of quartz. Crystals occur in granite veins in the Ural Mountains, Russia, and in basalt cavities in Brazil, Uruguay, and India.

Amethyst · Agate · Garnet · Pearl · Aquamarine · Agate · Amazonite

Rare beauty
This 19th-century gold box is set with a superb rare citrine surrounded by a stunning variety of other gems.

Rose quartz
Single crystals are rare. Most rose quartz is massive, best cut as cabochons (p. 59). Some can be polished to display a star.

Bacchus by Caravaggio
This 16th-century French verse tells how the god of wine rages that the first person he passes will be eaten by tigers. To save the beautiful maiden Amethyst, the goddess Diana turns her into a white stone. Regretting his anger, Bacchus pours red wine over the stone, turning it purple.

Impure of heart
Colorless rock crystal is the purest form of quartz. The many other colors are caused by impurities. Amethyst and citrine, for example, contain iron.

Massive

There are several massive varieties of quartz, made of tiny grains or fibers. Chalcedony—such as carnelian, chrysoprase, and agate—and jasper are distinguished by their grain patterns. Tiger's-eye and hawk's-eye form when asbestos is replaced by quartz and iron oxides.

Agate

Quartz grains in chalcedony occur in layers. Here, they progressively crystallized inward in a lava cavity.

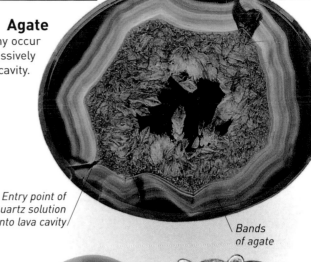

Entry point of quartz solution into lava cavity

Bands of agate

Tiger's-eye

This vein of tiger's-eye originally contained blue asbestos crystals. These were dissolved by solutions that deposited quartz and iron oxides in their place.

Polished tiger's-eye showing the eye effect called chatoyancy

A tiger shows why tiger's-eye is so named

Jasper

Interlocking quartz crystals in jasper are in a random mass with colorful impurities.

Vein of carnelian

Rock crystal

Carnelian

Most specimens of this translucent orange-red chalcedony result from heat-treating a less attractive chalcedony. This turns iron-bearing minerals into iron oxides, giving orange-red colors.

Chrysoprase

At its finest, chrysoprase is a vibrant green and the most valuable chalcedony. It has been used in ornaments and decorative patterns since prehistoric times.

Chrysoprase cameo set in gold

Diamond

Diamond crystal
Crystal system: cubic; hardness: 10; specific gravity: 3.5.

Derived from the Greek word *adamas* meaning "unconquerable," diamond is so-called because of its supreme hardness. Made of pure carbon with an immensely strong crystal structure (p. 14), evidence suggests that diamonds were formed 124 miles (200 km) deep within Earth. Discovered more than 2,000 years ago from river gravels in India, diamonds are now mined by about 20 countries. The top producer, Australia, supplies a quarter of the world's needs. A brilliant cut (p. 58) best reveals its luster and fire.

Diamond

Volcanic gemstone
This diamond is embedded in kimberlite, a volcanic rock first discovered in Kimberley, South Africa.

Rough diamonds
Rough diamonds mined from kimberlites often have lustrous crystal faces. Those from gravels can be dull because they get carried along in rough water with other rocks.

Mined diamonds

Alluvial diamonds

Diamonds

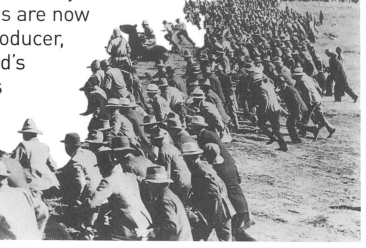

Diamond rush
In 1925, rich alluvial deposits were found at Lichtenburg, South Africa. The government allocated claims (areas to mine) on the outcome of a race—10,000 miners raced about 656 ft (200 m).

Spot the diamonds
In diamond-bearing gravels, seriously flawed stones are likely to be eroded away, so more of the diamonds found in gravels are of gem quality.

Unconquerable
Napoleon Bonaparte's sword was set with the Regent diamond. He hoped it would bring victory in battle because of an ancient belief that a diamond made its wearer unconquerable.

Rich mix
Conglomerate rock is a cemented mixture of rounded pebbles and mineral grains from water deposits. This South African specimen is rich in diamonds.

Indian diamond

Embedded in a sandy conglomerate, this rough diamond is from Hyderabad, India—the source of many famous large diamonds.

Valley of Diamonds

In this legendary valley, snakes guarded diamonds. A stranded Sindbad tied himself to meat thrown by a diamond collector. As intended, a bird rescued the meat, stuck with diamonds—and Sindbad!

Butterfly brooch

This brooch is set with more than 150 diamonds.

Diamonds are a girl's best friend

This movie song is from *Gentlemen Prefer Blondes*, in which Marilyn Monroe wears a yellow diamond called the Moon of Baroda.

Murchison snuff box

Set with diamonds and a portrait of Czar Alexander II of Russia, this gold box was presented to Sir Roderick Murchison in 1867 in recognition of his geological work in Russia.

Agnès Sorel (c.1422–1450)

Agnès Sorel, mistress of French king Charles VII, was the first in France to break the law made by Louis IX that only kings and nobles could wear diamonds.

Brilliant colors

Most natural diamonds are near-colorless; truly colorless ones are rare. A few are all colors in the spectrum (p. 16); good-quality ones are "fancies."

Famous diamonds

Some exceptional diamonds have long histories, while others have inspired fantastic legends.

The jewel in the crown

The Koh-i-noor, (mountain of light), is said to be the oldest large diamond, probably from India. Initially owned by Mogul kings, it was presented to Queen Victoria in 1850. Its cut (left) was unimpressive, so it was recut (p. 58).

Premier diamond

In 1905, the Cullinan crystal (actual size shown here) was mined in the Transvaal, South Africa, weighing 3,106 carats—the largest diamond ever found. In 1908, it was cut into smaller stones.

Blue Hope

The 45.52-carat Hope is famed for bringing bad luck. It is now in the Smithsonian Institution.

Corundum

Corundum
Crystal system: trigonal; hardness: 9; specific gravity: 3.96–4.05.

Corundum is an aluminum oxide, next to diamond in hardness, and is pleochroic (the color varies from different sides). Ruby and sapphire are varieties of it. Only true red stones are rubies, and sapphire indicates a blue stone, although other colors are called sapphire, such as pink sapphire. Most gems are found in gravels; the most famous are in Sri Lanka, Myanmar, and Kashmir. Australia is the largest producer of blue and golden sapphires.

Source revealed
A valley in the Zanskar range of the Himalayas in Kashmir is a famous source of fine sapphires, only revealed by an 1880s landslip.

Twin sapphire crystals

Kashmir blue
Kashmir has a reputation for sapphires of the finest blue. The term Kashmir blue describes sapphires of this color from elsewhere, too.

Sapphire intergrown with tourmaline

Myanmar crystal
Most quality rubies come from the Mogok region in Myanmar. Rubies from Myanmar, Pakistan, and Afghanistan are often found in calcite.

Ruskin's ruby
This 162-carat Myanmar ruby crystal was presented to the Natural History Museum, London, by philosopher John Ruskin in 1887. Its much-admired color is sometimes called "pigeon's blood" red.

Flattened prism of fine-quality ruby from the Mogok district of upper Myanmar

Bazaar dealing
This 1930 photograph shows ruby dealers in a Mogok bazaar. Gem-quality corundum is rare; ruby is the most valuable, fetching higher prices than diamonds.

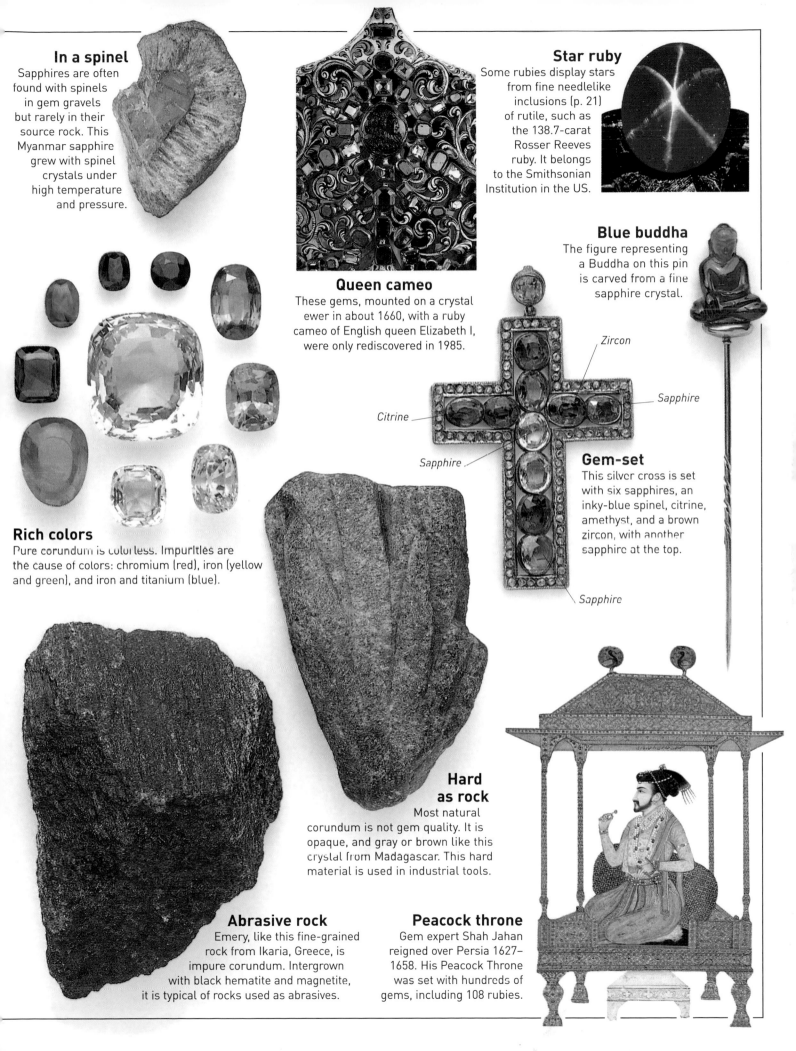

In a spinel

Sapphires are often found with spinels in gem gravels but rarely in their source rock. This Myanmar sapphire grew with spinel crystals under high temperature and pressure.

Queen cameo

These gems, mounted on a crystal ewer in about 1660, with a ruby cameo of English queen Elizabeth I, were only rediscovered in 1985.

Star ruby

Some rubies display stars from fine needlelike inclusions (p. 21) of rutile, such as the 138.7-carat Rosser Reeves ruby. It belongs to the Smithsonian Institution in the US.

Blue buddha

The figure representing a Buddha on this pin is carved from a fine sapphire crystal.

Zircon

Sapphire

Citrine

Sapphire

Gem-set

This silver cross is set with six sapphires, an inky-blue spinel, citrine, amethyst, and a brown zircon, with another sapphire at the top.

Sapphire

Rich colors

Pure corundum is colorless. Impurities are the cause of colors: chromium (red), iron (yellow and green), and iron and titanium (blue).

Hard as rock

Most natural corundum is not gem quality. It is opaque, and gray or brown like this crystal from Madagascar. This hard material is used in industrial tools.

Abrasive rock

Emery, like this fine-grained rock from Ikaria, Greece, is impure corundum. Intergrown with black hematite and magnetite, it is typical of rocks used as abrasives.

Peacock throne

Gem expert Shah Jahan reigned over Persia 1627–1658. His Peacock Throne was set with hundreds of gems, including 108 rubies.

Beryl

Popular for its durability and fine colors, beryl includes emerald (green), aquamarine (blue green), heliodor (yellow), and morganite (pink). Beryl is found in pegmatites (p. 25) and granites. In its massive, non-gem form, crystals can weigh as much as the 60-ft (18-m) Madagascan record holder at 40 tons (36 metric tons).

Beryl crystal
Crystal system: hexagonal; hardness: 7.5; specific gravity 2.63–2.91.

Russian host
A typical source of emeralds is mica schist, found in the early 1800s in the Ural Mountains, Russia.

Spanish spoils
The Colombian Chibcha Indians mined emeralds, which, through trade, reached the Incas in Peru and Aztecs in Mexico. In the early 1500s, the Spanish vowed to find their source, but did not find the Chivor mine until 1537; most of the emeralds sent to Spain were pillaged from the Incas.

Mined for life
The world's finest emeralds come from around Muzo and Chivor, Colombia. Many are mined and exported illegally.

1870 engraving of convicts working the Colombian emerald mines

Ancient mine
Emeralds were mined near the Red Sea in Egypt from 1500 BCE. The mines were rediscovered in 1816 but were unviable. This old entrance was discovered in about 1900.

Fine cut
This 911-carat, fine, cut aquamarine is owned by the US Smithsonian Institution.

Second-class crystal
A few emeralds are still found in Egypt in areas of granite, schist, and serpentine. Most crystals are blueish-green with many inclusions.

Color causes
Pure beryl is colorless. The reds and pinks are caused by manganese, the blues and yellows by iron, the emerald green by chromium or vanadium.

Sea green
Aquamarine means seawater and describes its color, caused by varying amounts of iron forms. It is fairly common, but its main source is in Brazil.

Morganite

Heliodor

Dry red
Red beryl is extremely rare and is the only natural beryl that contains no water in its structure. It occurs in "dry" volcanic rocks in the Western US.

Tourmaline inclusions

Gem belts
This large, gem-quality beryl crystal from Brazil is made up of zones of the varieties morganite and heliodor.

Turkish delight
The Topkapi Palace Treasury in Istanbul, Turkey, contains many pieces with fine emeralds, such as in the hilt of this 18th-century dagger.

Opal

Opal
Crystal system: amorphous or poorly crystalline; hardness: 5.5–6.5; specific gravity: 1.98–2.25.

The ancient Romans used opal as a symbol of power, but at times it has been considered unlucky. The Aztecs mined opal more than 500 years ago in Central America, which is still an important source, mainly of fire opal. The top producer of black and white opal is Australia. Opal is one of the few non-crystalline gems, and it has a tendency to crack and chip.

Roman source
This white opal piece is from Cervenica, Slovakia—the source used by the Romans and once part of Hungary. The opal here is said to be Hungarian.

The plague of venice
During the Black Death, depicted here by Antonio Zanchi, Venetians found opals unlucky—they brightened when a wearer caught the disease and dulled when they died.

Flash of lightning
The finest black opal is from Lightning Ridge, New South Wales, Australia. The color flashes are dramatic against its dark body, which, coupled with its rarity, makes it more valuable than white opal.

Not flashy
Nonprecious opal without flashes of color is called potch. Rose opal is potch, but it is popular for decorative jewelry. This specimen comes from France; other sources are in Idaho.

Australian fair
The major Australian opal deposits occur in sedimentary rocks in the Great Artesian Basin. Famous mines include White Cliffs, Lightning Ridge, and Coober Pedy.

Glassy look
This clear, glassy looking opal (hyalite) from Bohemia occurs in volcanic-lava cavities. Those with a play of color are the prized water opal. Hydrophane is opaque but appears colorless in water.

Greatly enlarged photograph of precious opal, showing the ordered silica spheres

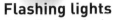

Flashing lights
Precious opal has flashes of color, dependent on its structural silica-sphere sizes. Opal with a dark background is called black; others, white.

On the map
"Prospector's brooches" in the shape of Australia marked the arrival on the market in the late 1800s of Australian opal.

Opal cameo *Dawn with Cupid and Psyche* in the Natural History Museum, London, UK

Mexican fire
Mexico is famous for its fire opal—a nearly transparent variety, still showing flashes of color, from yellow to orange and red.

Moved in
The opal localities in Australia are very hot. When mines are worked out, the near-surface excavations are adapted into cool living spaces.

Precious fossil
Opal often replaces bones and shells of animals, plus wood tissue, as in this wood from Nevada. It grows bit by bit to replace the original material in fossils.

Boulder opal
If this hardened sandy clay with iron oxides and precious-opal layers has enough iron, the rock is dark and opal surfaces can be carved into cameos.

Precious opal   *Potch opal*

Opal fruit
This was an aggregate of radiating crystals of glauberite but has been replaced by precious opal. Found in Australia, this type of opal is popularly known as "pineapple opal."

Drunk driving
French king Louis XIV named his coaches after gemstones. The driver of the *Opal* was usually drunk, as shown in this picture detail of a painting by Van der Meulen, and so opal and the coach were thought to be unlucky!

Other gemstones

A gemstone's properties are beauty, rarity, and durability. In addition to those detailed on previous pages, gems found in jewelery stores include topaz, tourmaline, garnet, and peridot. Some, such as kunzite, sphene, and fluorite, are so soft or rare they are cut only for collectors.

Marvelous gems
"Fishing for pearls and gathering turquoises" from *The Book of Marvels* by Marco Polo.

Topaz crystal
Crystal system: orthorhombic; hardness: 8; specific gravity: 3.52–3.56.

Topaz

The history of topaz, before it was named in the early 18th century, is unclear. Its name is said to come from *Topazius*, Greek for Zabargad—an island in the Red Sea.

Crystal fame
This pale-blue crystal is from Brazil—the most famous topaz source. Other sources include the US, Japan, and Russia.

Plane of cleavage

Needs protection
Although very hard, topaz can be easily broken because it has one direction of perfect cleavage (p. 15), seen clearly in this crystal. Any jewelry setting for topaz must therefore be protective.

One of the best
The best golden topaz, such as this prism, is from Ouro Prêto, Brazil. Some gems show color from golden brown to pink. Pink gems are called imperial topaz.

Topaz tricks
Topaz is sometimes mistaken for diamond. Both are often found in gravel, and they have a similar specific gravity.

Topaz colors
An aluminum silicate of about 20 percent water and fluorine, topaz that has more water is golden brown or pink; with more fluorine it is blue or colorless.

Brazilian Princess
This 21,327-carat topaz was cut in 1977. The largest cut stone today is 36,853 carats.

Tourmaline

This mineral's complex chemistry crystallizes as prisms with flat or wedge-shaped ends. Every crystal has a different structure at each end, giving it an electrical property. If a crystal is warmed, one end becomes positively charged and the other negatively charged.

Tourmaline crystal
Crystal system: trigonal; hardness: 7–7.5; specific gravity: 3–3.25.

John Ruskin (1819–1900)
Ruskin wrote:"The chemistry of tourmaline is more like a medieval doctor's prescription than the making of a respectable mineral!"

Framed up
This tourmaline prism slice shows threefold symmetry and a triangular cross-section. The color zones indicate that it was built up in layers.

Black and green
Tourmaline is pleochroic, which means it is a different color when viewed down different axes (pp. 12–13).

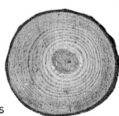

Crystal growth rings of some crystals can be similar to those of tree trunks

Strange attachment
This tourmaline is unusually attached to quartz by a prism face. The pink prism crystallized first, then green tourmaline formed the ends.

Tourmaline crystal

Cut stone of two colors of "watermelon" tourmaline

Set in granite
Gem-quality tourmalines, such as in Brazil, are most often found in pegmatite veins (p. 25) or granites.

Tourmaline crystal

Multicolored
Tourmaline shows great color range. Even some individual crystals, such as "watermelon," are more than one color.

Garnet crystals

Crystal system: cubic; hardness: 6.5–7.5; specific gravity: 3.52–4.32.

Ring set with almandine garnet

Garnet

Garnet is a family of chemically related minerals including almandine, pyrope, spessartine, grossular, and andradite. They can all be found as gemstones; almandine-pyrope is the most widely used. The different chemical compositions mean garnet occurs in most colors other than blue. Sources include Slovakia and South Africa.

Cut pyrope garnet

Pyrope

This deep-red garnet is mostly found in Bohemia (Czech Republic).

Cut demantoid garnet

Demantoid

This emerald-green garnet is the most prized, found in the Ural Mountains, Russia.

Spessartine cabochon

Spessartine

These beautiful orange colors are caused by manganese. Gem-quality crystals are rare.

Fruity name

Almandine-pyrope gems are pomegranate color; "garnet" may be from the Latin for the fruit.

Almandine

Garnet commonly crystallizes as icositetrahedrons, like these almandine crystals. Due to its deep color, almandine is often cut as cabochons (p. 59).

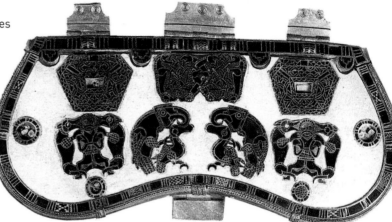

Fit for a king

This 7th-century purse lid was among many garnet-set pieces found in an Anglo-Saxon royal burial ship in Sutton Hoo, Suffolk, England.

Andradite

Most andradite garnet is not gem-quality. Only demantoid, topazolite, and melanite (this black variety), are used as gemstones.

Cut grossular garnets

Grossular

Some grossular garnet looks like gooseberries, and the name may come from *grossularia*, which is Latin for gooseberry. This pink grossular from Mexico shows dodecahedral crystals, one of garnet's two main habits.

Color traces

Green grossular contains vanadium; yellow and red contain iron. The red variety is hessonite.

Peridot crystal
Crystal system: orthorhombic; hardness: 6.5; specific gravity: 3.22–3.40.

Cut peridot from Arizona

Cut peridot from Norway

Cut peridot from Myanmar

Peridot suppliers
Zabargad and Myanmar produce the largest; Arizona, Hawaii, and Norway supply fine gems.

Ring set with peridot

Peridot
This French word may come from the Arabic *faridat*—"a gem." Peridot is the gem variety of olivine, a magnesium and iron silicate, common in volcanic rocks.

Olivine-rich rock

Lava

Volcanic bomb
This solidified lava with fragments of olivine-rich rock from deep within Earth was ejected through a volcano.

Island gem
Peridot usually occurs intergrown with other minerals. Crystals with distinct faces (right) come from Zabargad island in the Red Sea.

Name change
Peridot mines have long existed on Zabargad in the Red Sea. The stones from here were known by the Ancient Greeks as topazos (p. 42).

Sunstone
The bright spangles in sunstones are reflections from tiny dark-red flakes of hematite.

The stones' namesakes, the Sun and the Moon

Moonstone
This gem is from the potash-rich feldspar group. The other feldspar group is rich in soda and calcium, and includes sunstone. Feldspars are common but rarely gem-quality, ranging in hardness from 6–6.5 and in specific gravity from 2.56–2.76.

Moonstone
This pegmatitic feldspar from Myanmar shows the moonstone sheen. Pegmatites (p. 25) may be the source of moonstones from Sri Lankan and Indian gem gravels.

Blue moon
Most moonstones are colorless with a bluish sheen. Some are gray (which may show good cat's-eyes, p. 59), orange pink, yellow, or pale green.

Pin set with sunstone

Ring set with moonstone

Spinel

Red and blue spinels can rival ruby and sapphire in richness. Until the 19th century, when scientist Romé de l'Isle (p. 12) distinguished true ruby from red spinel, red spinels were confusingly called balas rubies. "Balas" may relate to a source in Balascia, now called Badakhshan, in Afghanistan.

Princely reward
England's "Black Prince" Edward was given a balas ruby for helping King Peter of Castile, Spain, win the Battle of Najera in 1367.

Spinel crystal
Crystal system: cubic; hardness: 8; specific gravity: 3.5–3.7.

Polished over
This crystal has been polished to remove surface blemishes, but still has its octahedral shape.

Small distortion
Spinel usually crystallizes as octahedra, but this crystal aggregate has small distorted octahedra in parallel growth.

Black Prince's ruby

Cullinan II diamond

Reformed character
This rock from Lake Baikal, Russia, contains octahedra of blue spinel in a matrix of white calcite and muscovite mica. It was probably an impure limestone that recrystallized.

Lying in state
The Black Prince's balas ruby (a 170-carat spinel) is now in the British Imperial State Crown above another famous stone, the Cullinan II diamond (p. 35).

Travelers
Most gems, such as these from Myanmar, are from gravels. The gems are not very worn, which shows they did not travel far.

Thorny crystals
These crystallized octahedra from Bodenmais, Germany, are gahnite, a zinc-rich spinel variety. They show spinel's thornlike triangular crystal faces, suggesting its name is from the Latin for thorn—*spina*.

Crystal colors
Pure spinel is colorless. The reds and pinks here are due to chromium in the crystals.

Zircon

Named from the Arabic *zargoon* (golden), zircon comes from Sri Lanka, Thailand, Brazil, and Australia. Colorless zircon looks like diamond in luster and fire, but it is softer and may look "sleepy" because of inclusions and double refraction (p. 18).

Red zircon was once known as hyacinth

Natural colors

Zircon is zirconium silicate, colorless when pure, but found in a wide range of colors due to different impurities.

Zircon crystal
Crystal system: tetragonal; hardness 7.5; specific gravity: 4.6–4.7.

Radioactive

This large pebble from Sri Lanka is a typical zircon color. Some zircons contain so much uranium and thorium that radioactivity breaks down the crystal structure, making the stone amorphous, or non-crystalline.

Heat treatment

Heating red-brown zircon crystals in an oxygen-free atmosphere produces blue zircon; heating in air (with oxygen) produces a golden color; a colorless crystal can be produced by both methods. These colors may fade, but reheating can restore them.

Natural brown zircon crystals

Heat-treated blue zircon

Stones cut from heat-treated zircon

Chrysoberyl

Only diamond and corundum exceed the gem chrysoberyl in hardness. The yellow, green, and brown colors are caused by iron or chromium. The three varieties are: clear yellow-green gems, cat's-eye or cymophane, and alexandrite, famous for its dramatic color change. The best chrysoberyl comes from Russia.

Russian alexandrite

Discovered in 1830 in the Ural Mountains on Czar Alexander II's birthday (hence the name), alexandrite looks green by day and red in artificial light—Russia's imperial colors.

Cut yellow chrysoberyl

Cut alexandrite

Popular in Portugal
Yellow-green chrysoberyls from Brazil became popular in Portuguese jewelry.

Chrysoberyl crystal
Crystal system: orthorhombic; hardness: 8.5; specific gravity: 3.68–3.78.

Collectors' items

There are more than 3,000 mineral species, but crucial factors such as hardness (pp. 18–19), durability, and rarity reduce the number of commercial gems to about 30. Many people collect rare gems of exceptional size or color, or cut minerals that are too soft or fragile for jewelry, such as blende and sphene. Benitoite, on the other hand, is durable but rare.

Axinite
Beautiful wedge-shaped crystals of brown axinite from Bourg d'Oisans, France, display gray and violet flashes in different directions. Once very rare, more crystals are being found in Sri Lanka.

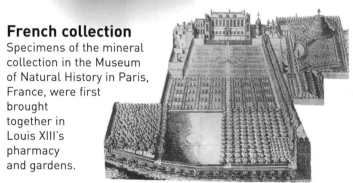

Sphene
Ranging from yellow-brown to emerald-green, sphene has great luster and fire but is soft. The finest gems come from US, the Swiss Alps, and Myanmar.

French collection
Specimens of the mineral collection in the Museum of Natural History in Paris, France, were first brought together in Louis XIII's pharmacy and gardens.

Alpine experts
Many fine Alpine crystals are collected by strahlers— experienced mountaineers who are talented mineral collectors.

Tanzanite
This gem variety of zoisite, found in 1967 in Tanzania, is rare for its blue, magenta, and yellow-gray displays. Many greenish-gray crystals are heat-treated to become blue.

Danburite
This mineral was first found as colorless crystals in a pegmatite (p. 25) in Danbury, Connecticut (hence its name). More colorless stones come from Japan and Mexico.

Cordierite
Showing very strong pleochroism, from blue to yellowish-gray, this gem was used by the Vikings to navigate their long boats (p. 60), which is why they are called "water sapphires." Gem-quality cordierite comes from Sri Lanka, Myanmar, Madagascar, and India.

Benitoite

These crystals from, and named for, San Benito County, California, are comparable in color to fine sapphires and display similar fire to diamonds, but are very rare.

The San Benito Mine in 1914 showing the open cut and an ore bucket on the left

Blende
Sphalerite, or blende, is the world's major source of zinc. It is normally opaque gray to black, but gem-quality yellow, green, and reddish-brown crystals come from Mexico and Spain. They are, however, too soft for jewelry.

Blende crystals in matrix   Rough blende crystal

Cut kunzite

Cut pale-green spodumene

Kunzite crystal

Spodumene
Magnificent spodumene crystals come from Brazil, California, and Afghanistan. Fine gems are cut from pale-green, yellow, and pink crystals—the latter, kunzite, is named after G. F. Kunz. Rare, green hiddenite is found in North Carolina and Sri Lanka.

George Frederick Kunz worked for New York jeweler Tiffany's

Goldney grotto
Precious stones and corals cover the walls and pillars of this underground grotto, built 1737–1764 near Bristol, England.

Scapolite
These gems occur in pastel shades of pink, yellow, purple, and fine cat's-eyes (p. 59).

Sinhalite
Thought to be Sri Lankan peridot, sinhalite was proved in 1950 to be a new species and named after an old name for Sri Lanka—Sinhala.

Fibrolite
This 19.84-carat rare variety of the mineral sillimanite is from Myanmar. It is one of the world's biggest. Andalusite is also made of aluminum silicate but has a different structure—gem-quality stones from Brazil and Sri Lanka show pleochroic red and green.

Cut fibrolite

Cut andalusite

Malachite
This vivid green copper mineral is 4 on the hardness scale (pp. 18–19); specific gravity is 3.8. The Democratic Republic of Congo, Zambia, Australia, and Russia are main sources.

Stones for carving

Microcrystalline rocks and minerals have been used in decoration for thousands of years. Jade, turquoise, and lapis were used for jewelry and carvings in ancient civilizations, such as ancient Egypt, China, and Sumeria.

Turquoise tradition
Most turquoise comes from the US southwest and is often used in traditional Native-American jewelry.

Lapis lazuli

This is not a single mineral but a rock of blue lazurite with variable amounts of calcite and pyrite. The best, from Afghanistan, is mostly lazurite, a deep blue, and 5.5 in hardness, with a specific gravity of 2.7–2.9. Other sources exist in Russia and Chile.

White calcite

Persian blue
The name lapis lazuli is derived from the Persian word for blue. Its color is caused by sulfur.

Turquoise

Turquoise occurs in nodules and veins of green or blue: copper makes it blue, while iron makes it green. It has a specific gravity of 2.6–2.9 and a hardness of 5–6.

Natural mosaic
Turquoise most often occurs in mosaics. The finest blue turquoise comes from Iran (previously Persia).

Popular jewel
Lapis lazuli has been used for beads and other jewelry.

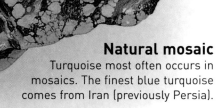

Blue Persian turquoise inlaid with gold

Ancient skull
This mask of turquoise and lignum, shaped around a human skull, was made by the ancient Aztec civilization.

Medieval painting
Lapis lazuli was crushed and purified in medieval times to make the paint pigment ultramarine, used in the Wilton Diptych altar piece (shown here).

Jade

The Spanish conquerors of Mexico believed the Native peoples' green stones would cure kidney ailments. They called them kidney stones, or *piedra de hyada*, which is where the word jade was derived. In 1863, the stones were proven to be two different minerals, now called jadeite and nephrite.

Life jacket
The ancient Chinese believed jade could give life and so placed plates of nephrite around a corpse to try to preserve it. This is a 2nd-century-BCE funeral suit of a princess.

Jadeite
Mainly found in Myanmar, jadeite varies widely in color. The most prized is the emerald-green jadeite known as imperial jade. Jadeite has a hardness of 6.5–7 and a specific gravity of 3.3–3.5.

Jadeite fashioned into a ball

Nephrite design by Russian jeweler, Fabergé

Chinese camel
This nephrite camel was carved in China. White and cream nephrites contain very little iron. More iron causes green and black stones.

Nephrite
Used by the Maoris of New Zealand, it has a hardness of 6.5 and specific gravity of 2.9–3.1.

Rhodonite
Rhodo means pink; its color is caused by manganese. It has a hardness of about 6 and is used for carving and inlays.

Other stones

Many other stones are popular for carving, mainly because of their color. These include malachite, Blue John, serpentine, and rhodonite.

Serpentine
Carvers can use the snake-skin patterns in serpentine for works of art. Some is soft and easy to carve, but the yellow-green bowenite, favored by Chinese carvers, is up to 6 in hardness.

Blue John
This purple and pale-yellow banded fluorite comes from Derbyshire, England. It is fragile, so is usually bonded with resins to make it durable.

19th-century Blue John vase

Precious metals

Gold, silver, and platinum are crystalline, although single crystals are rare. Gold and silver were among the earliest metals worked, but today platinum is more valuable. All three are relatively soft, easy to work, difficult to destroy, and have high SGs (p. 18).

Gold Rush
The desire for gold has long driven people to journey far and wide. In 1848, gold seekers rushed to California. Most gold was recovered from placer deposits by panning (p. 25).

Well placed
These placer deposits of erosion debris from gold-bearing rock show small particles of gold.

Gold

Gold is used for measuring wealth. Pure gold (24 carats) is a dense (SG = 19.3) but soft (H = 2.5–3) metal. Before it can be used, it has to be refined, and it is often alloyed with other metals to make it harder.

Latrobe nugget
This crystalline gold nugget was found in 1855 in the presence of His Excellency C. J. Latrobe, Governor of the colony of Victoria, Australia.

Gold sandwich
Gold is sometimes found in hydrothermal veins, associated with quartz, as in this quartz vein from New Zealand.

Worth its weight
The golden Buddha of Bangkok is 6 tons (5.5 metric tons) of gold, worth over $50 million.

Built on gold
The Asante Kingdom (producers of this lion ring) dominated what is now Ghana in 1700–1900, its power founded upon its gold resources.

Rare sight
Gold usually occurs as fine grains scattered throughout a rock, or as "invisible gold," making this group of crystals from Zimbabwe very rare.

Platinum

Platinum is used in modern technology, as a standard weight, for surgical instruments, and in jewelry. Its name means little silver. Platinum is often found in granules or small nuggets in placer deposits in Russia, Canada, and South Africa.

Rounded
Platinum is quite soft (H = 4–4.5); it is unusual to find sharp crystals.

Platinum crown
The crown of Queen Elizabeth the Queen Mother was made of platinum.

Rich layer
This platinum-bearing pyroxenite comes from igneous rock in South Africa called the Merensky reef. It is only 12 in (30 cm) thick but is rich in platinum.

Unusually large
This 2.4-lb (1.1-kg) nugget of platinum from the Ural Mountains, Russia, is unusually large.

Silver mine
In medieval times, Sainte Marie area, Alsace, France, was one of the richest silver-mining areas in Europe. Here, miners are removing silver ore.

Silver

Silver crystals are rare, but cubic crystals have been found. Silver usually occurs massive or as thick, wiry aggregates. It has a hardness of 2.5–3. In medieval times, silver was more valuable than gold. Today, metallic silver is used in electronics and photography (p. 63).

In need of polishing
This dendritic growth (p. 23) of silver crystals from Chile is slightly tarnished.

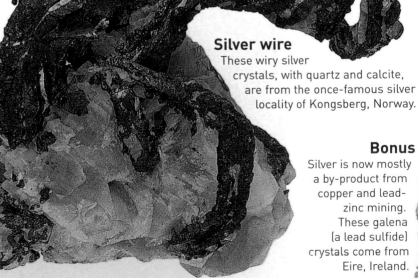

Silver wire
These wiry silver crystals, with quartz and calcite, are from the once-famous silver locality of Kongsberg, Norway.

Bonus
Silver is now mostly a by-product from copper and lead-zinc mining. These galena (a lead sulfide) crystals come from Eire, Ireland.

Organic gems

Gems from animals and plants, such as amber, jet, coral, pearl, and shell, are called organic. They are not as hard (4 or less) or as dense (1.04—amber to 2.78—pearl) as gemstones but are popular because of their beauty. Pearls have long been valued, while shell and amber have been found in ancient graves from 2000 BCE.

Prehistoric gems
In the Jurassic period, dinosaurs lived among the trees that produced amber and jet.

Jet and amber

Jet and amber both come from trees. Jet is a fine-grained, black rock formed over millions of years from rotted and compressed trees. Amber is the fossilized resin, or sap, of trees.

Jet lagged
This jet contains fossils of several long-extinct animals, including an ammonite. Jet is hard-wearing and can be polished.

Fossil ammonite

Ancient traveler
The south and east coasts of the Baltic sea are major sources of amber, which is slightly denser than seawater and can be carried across the sea.

Coral

Coral is a skeleton of calcium carbonate made by colonies of animals in tropical waters. The range of colors is due to different growth conditions and organic contents.

Carving from Mediterranean coral of a monkey on a branch

Coral living in a tropical sea

Ancient values
This highly prized red coral from the Mediterranean is *Corallium rubrum*.

Necklace material
From the species *Heliopora caerules*, this blue coral grows around the Philippines. It is often cut into beads.

Pearl and shell

The sheen on pearls and some shells is caused by light reflecting on tiny platelets of calcium called nacre. Pearls form in shells when a foreign body gets stuck in the shell and the animal surrounds it with nacre.

Oyster catchers

For more than 2,000 years, the Persian Gulf has supplied pearls, recovered by divers. Today, an irritant is put into oysters and shells are farmed for pearls.

Pearls of color

Pearls' many colors include yellow, pink, and cream.

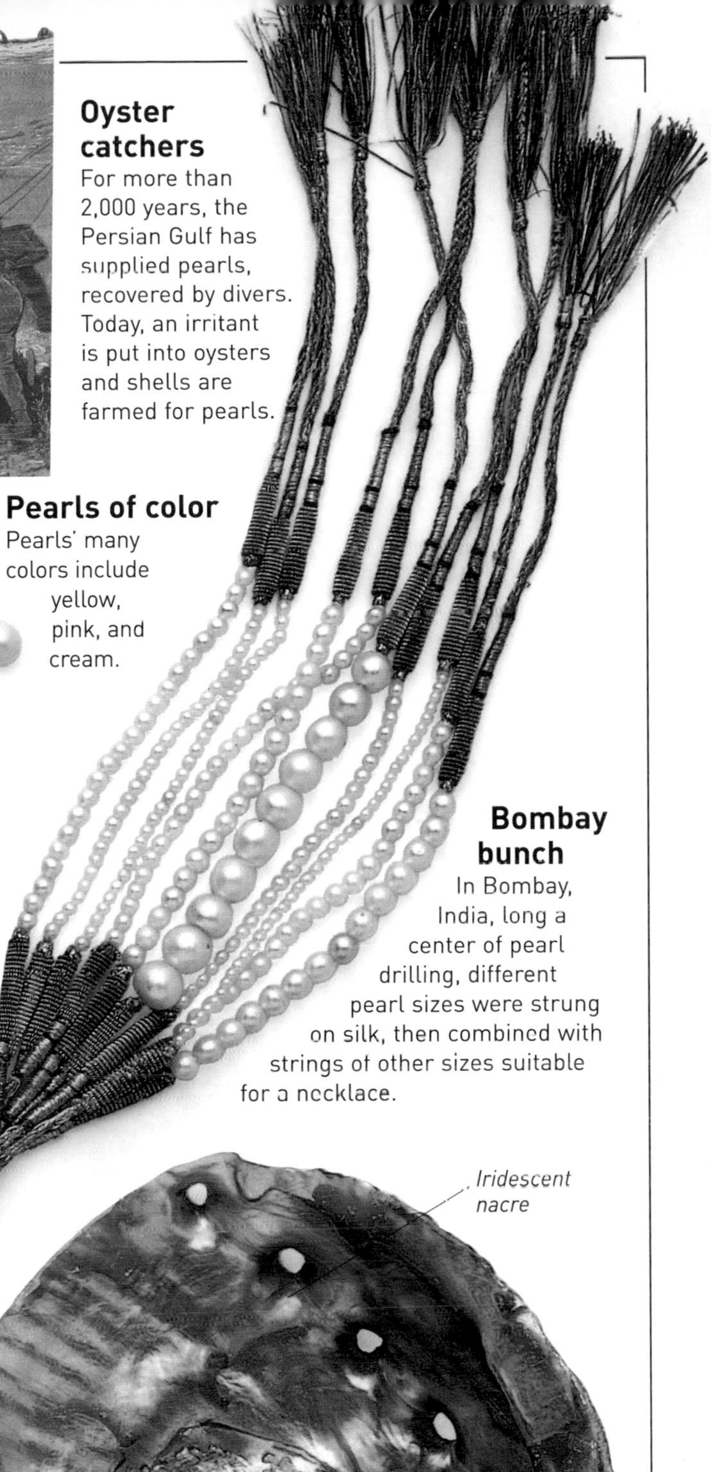

Bombay bunch

In Bombay, India, long a center of pearl drilling, different pearl sizes were strung on silk, then combined with strings of other sizes suitable for a necklace.

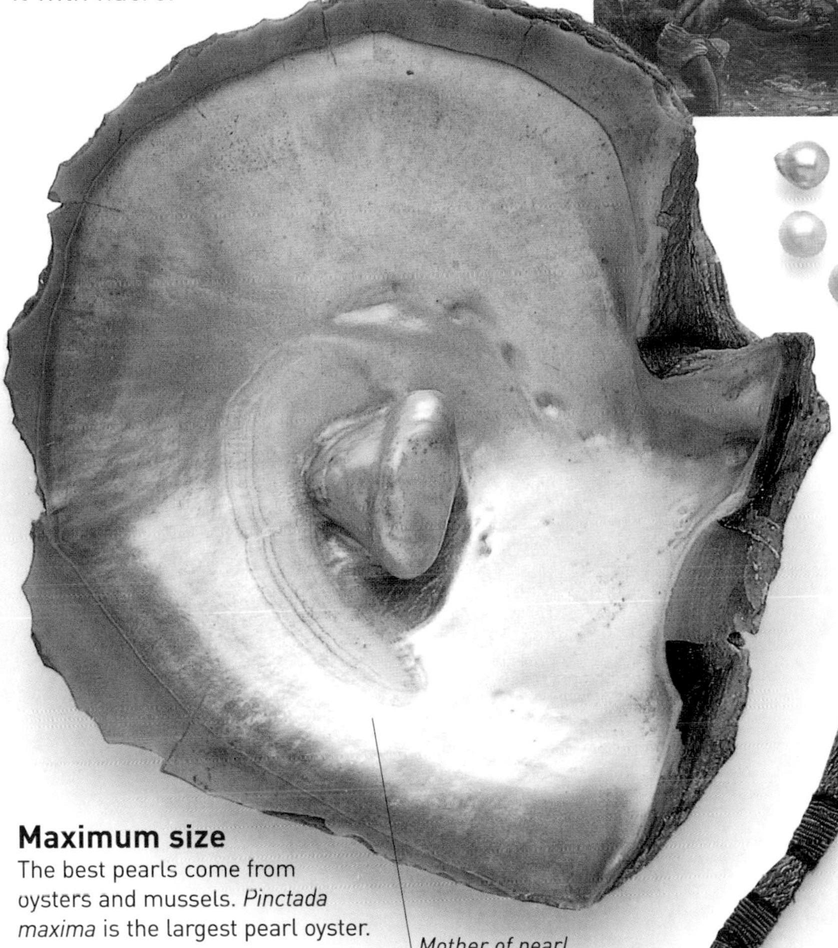

Iridescent nacre

Maximum size

The best pearls come from oysters and mussels. *Pinctada maxima* is the largest pearl oyster.

Mother of pearl

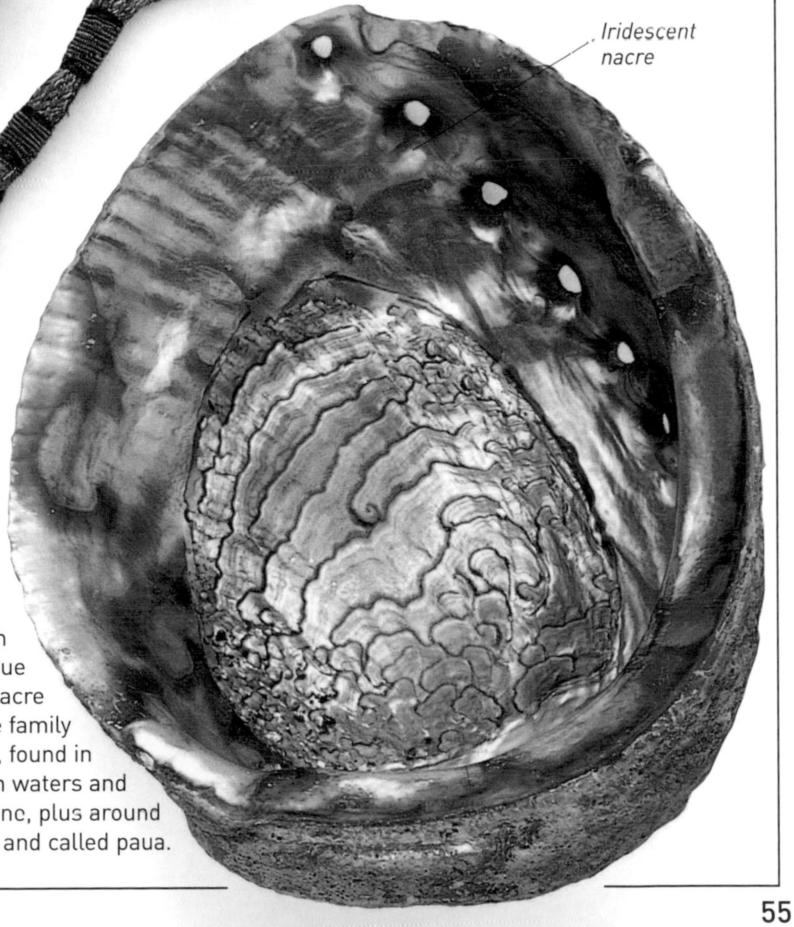

Canning jewel

Irregularly shaped pearls are called baroque pearls. Four, including one forming the body, are in the Canning Triton jewel, probably made in the late 16th century in south Germany.

Baroque pearl

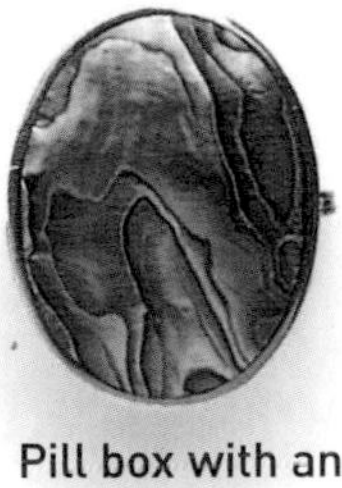

Pill box with an abalone lid

Shiny

Shells with bright blue and green nacre belong to the family *Haliotis*, found in American waters and called abalone, plus around New Zealand and called paua.

What is it worth?

The market value of gems plays a large part in persuading people to buy them, but fashions change over time. During the 5th through 14th centuries, stones were often not cut because this was thought to destroy their magic. Now, stones are cut to enhance their beauty, and they are traded so people can display their style or wealth. Ruby, pearl, emerald, diamond, and sapphire have been popular since medieval times.

What price?
Gem values can vary, even within one species. This 57.26-carat sapphire is of such size and fine color that it can only be valued if it changes hands.

Baptiste Tavernier
This Frenchman traveled Europe and Asia in the 17th century, trading gems. His detailed journals are used to research famous diamonds.

Cut synthetic ruby

1-carat ruby

Carob seed

Carob pod

Priceless
Painite is priceless and very few crystals have been found. It was discovered in Myanmar by gem dealer A. C. D. Pain and was named after him.

Weight in beans
Carob tree seeds are constant in weight and were long used as a standard for comparing gem weight. Later, a standard weight similar to the carob seed's was used—the carat—for which, early in the 20th century, a metric standard of 0.2 g (0.007 oz) was agreed to internationally.

Synthetic ruby crystals

Chipped glass of a GTD

Not cheap
Growing synthetic crystals (pp. 26–27) is expensive. Stones cut from them are therefore not cheap, but natural stones still cost 10 to 100 times more.

Doubled up
A stone made of two materials fused together is known as a doublet. In the popular garnet-topped doublet (GTD), the top is a thin piece of colorless garnet, which is more durable than the color-providing glass base. These cheaper stones are sometimes sold by disreputable traders as rubies, sapphires, or emeralds.

Theft prevention
This 1910 photograph shows Chinese sorters in the Mogok ruby mines, Myanmar, wearing wire hoods to stop them from putting rubies in their mouths and stealing.

Short-lasting
Red glass is used to imitate ruby, but its luster and shape fade. Ruby's hardness and toughness keeps its qualities for longer.

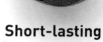

Strontium
titanate

Synthetic
rutile

Fluorite

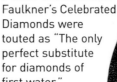
Quartz

Fake diamonds
Faulkner's Celebrated Diamonds were touted as "The only perfect substitute for diamonds of first water."

Lithium
niobate

Stone substitutes
Diamond is the most frequently imitated stone in jewelry. The oldest imitations are glass and rock crystal, but in the 20th century synthetic versions became available. These diamond simulants are arranged clockwise, from fluorite, in order of increasing fire.

Topaz

Cubic
zirconia

Synthetic
sapphire

GGG (gadolinium
gallium garnet)

Diamond

Synthetic
spinel

YAG (yttrium
aluminum
garnet)

Zircon

Glass

Clarity and color are graded on a scale. This diamond is graded SI$_1$ (small inclusion) for clarity and G (near colorless) for color.

Details of proportions, clarity, and color are listed

SAMPLE

Money man
Valuable stones sell for lots of money, but the most expensive diamond on the market was only a fraction of the price paid for Van Gogh's *Portrait of Dr. Gachet*, sold at Christies, New York, in May 1990 for $82.5 million.

Four Cs
Two diamonds that look alike can have different values. The four Cs are characteristics that determine value: cut, weight in carats, color, and clarity. In the 1930s, the Gemological Institute of America established a grading system, issuing certificates with information about the four Cs for each diamond. Europe had different systems, but in 1975 the grading procedure was standardized.

The positions of any inclusions are indicated on the outlines of the crown and pavilion

Made to match
True opal is graded according to body color and the play of colors. Black opal is rare and the most expensive. Opal is imitated in several ways. Slocum stone is glass and much cheaper; Gilson opal is grown in the laboratory and is intermediate in value.

Polystyrene
latex

Real black opal

Gilson opal

Slocum
stone

Cutting gems

Some crystals are beautiful in shape, luster, and color, but most are imperfect. A lapidary (skilled polisher and stone cutter) can turn them into valuable objects of beauty. Beads and cabochons are old cuts, such as for turquoise (p. 50). Today, brilliant-cut diamonds are the most popular form.

Brilliant-cut rutile
In 1919, Marcel Tolkowsky set the specifications of a brilliant cut to give the best sparkle, brilliance, and fire.

Rose-cut smoky quartz
Dating from the 14th century, the rose cut has a flat base and a dome-shaped top covered in triangular facets.

Table-cut amethyst
The top is sawed off the octahedron to achieve this cut.

Step-cut quartz
This cut has many rectangular facets, suitable for strongly colored gems.

Cutting a brilliant

A lapidary first studies a rough stone with a loupe (powerful lens) to find any flaws. The stone is marked to show where it should be sawn and the facets are ground.

Crown

Bezel

1 Choice
A rough crystal is chosen.

2 Sawn in two
The crystal is sawn to remove the top pyramid and rounded by grinding against another diamond, called bruting.

Girdle

Pavilion

Table facet

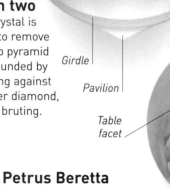

Brilliant recut
The Koh-i-noor diamond (p. 35) was recut into a brilliant in 1852. Here, the Duke of Wellington makes the first facet, with Amsterdam cutter Mr. Voorsanger.

3 Faceting begins
The stone is mounted on a dop (stick) and the flat table facet is ground on a scaife (cast-iron wheel).

Koh-i-noor brilliant cut

Petrus Beretta
In the 17th century, Amsterdam became the world center for trading and cutting diamonds. It held a prominent position until the 1930s.

4 Further facets
Three sets of four bezel facets are ground: between the table and girdle, on the pavilion, on the crown, plus a culet facet on the base.

5 Finished off
A brillianteer adds 24 facets above and 16 below the girdle. A standard brilliant has 57 facets (58 with a culet).

Diamond cutter's table of the 1870s

Agate

Amethyst

Beads

This fashioned gem form can be made with soft materials. Today they are made with machines.

Cutting it fine

Diamond-cutting tools of the 15th century were only replaced with the development of automatic machines in the 1970s, and, later, lasers (seen here, in Australia).

Triangular-cut citrine

Irregular-cut sapphire

Heart-cut heliodor

Special cuts

A special cut may be developed for a rare stone, to keep its weight, or for special occasions.

Hard-headed

Hard-wearing opaque materials such as this garnet are often cut as cabochons—rounds or ovals with plain, curved surfaces.

Light display

Star sapphires and rubies (p. 37) are cut as cabochons for the rutile to reflect the light and show the star.

Quartz cabochons in a brooch, cut to display the cat's-eye effect

Groove caused by polishing garnet cabochons

Over and over

Tumbling rocks and minerals in a drum with water and grit (coarse grit to start, fine grit to finish) polishes them.

Indian polish

This massive corundum was used in India in the 19th century for fashioning and polishing garnets. Over time, tiny chips split off, eventually leaving grooves.

Grinding

Stones are held against large, water-driven grinding wheels in this 20th-century agate-grinding workshop.

Lore and legend

Superstition and myth have long been attached to crystals. In Persian mythology, the world is said to stand on a giant sapphire, coloring the skies blue. Emeralds were once thought to blind snakes, diamonds to be medicinal, and rubies were symbols of power in the Middle Ages. Some crystals are said to be cursed, bringing disaster to their owners.

Crystal compass
The Vikings may have navigated with transparent cordierite crystals. When held up to sunlight and rotated, cordierite darkens and changes color, which could be used to work out compass directions.

Migrating birds
A magnetic crystal in birds' brains may detect the Earth's magnetic field.

Power to repel
Some pieces of magnetite (an iron oxide), are magnetic. Known as lodestones, they were once believed to have special powers; Alexander the Great gave lodestones to his soldiers to repel evil spirits.

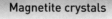

Iron filings attracted to magnetite follow magnetic lines of force

Magnetite crystals

Sobering influence
In the 15th century, amethyst was believed to cure drunkenness. This may be because drinking vessels were sometimes made of amethyst, and made water look like red wine, and so had no intoxicating effect!

Holy rows
The original breastplate of the High Priest of Israel is described in the Bible (Exodus 28,15–30) as set with four rows of three stones. The stones are all named but some are misleading. The sapphire, for example, is actually lapis lazuli.

Stone tears
Staurolite crystals can twin at right angles to form crosses, and were used as amulets at baptisms. Those in Patrick County, Virginia, are called fairy stones from the legend that they crystallized from the sad tears of fairies upon Christ's death.

Crystal gazing

Crystal balls have been used for telling the future since Greek and Roman times. The fortune-teller gazes at the polished surface until they can no longer focus on the ball but see instead a curtain of mist, enabling "visions" to be seen, imagined for the person whose fortune is being told.

Visionary
John Dee, a 16th-century charlatan but a favorite of England's Queen Elizabeth I, conducted many crystal gazings.

For the future
Quartz is the most popular material for crystal balls, but other materials with a shiny surface have been used.

Eastern promiser
Crystal balls have been found in the Far East, Americas, and Europe.

Birthstones

A special stone dedicated to each month of the year was first suggested in the 1st century CE, linked to the 12 stones in the High Priest's breastplate. Wearing such stones became popular in the 18th century, first in Poland.

In the cards
Signs of the zodiac were also given their own gemstones. In these 1923 cigarette cards, carnelian represents Virgo, and peridot represents Leo.

December
(Turquoise)

January
(Garnet)

February
(Amethyst)

November
(Topaz)

October
(Opal)

March
(Aquamarine)

September
(Sapphire)

April
(Diamond)

Rock crystal engraved with the 12 signs of the zodiac

May
(Emerald)

August
(Peridot)

July
(Ruby)

June
(Pearl)

Changes
The gem for each month varied over time, with different Roman, Arabian, Jewish, and Russian combinations. The group here is popular today.

At home

Many items at home are crystalline including ice crystals in the freezer, salt crystals in food, and silicon crystal chips in the fridge and washing machine. The TV and camera work thanks to crystals, the house is built of crystalline materials, and cars stand outside, slowly rusting—crystallizing!

By a whisker
In this early form of wireless, a thin copper wire, called a cat's whisker, was moved against a galena crystal to pick up radio waves. These crystal sets became popular in the 1920s.

For the record
In some record players, the stylus is hard-wearing diamond or corundum, and a piezoelectric crystal (p. 31) converts vibrations into an electrical charge.

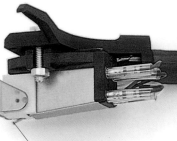

Diamond stylus

Enlarged photograph of a diamond stylus traveling on a record groove

Spoonful of sugar
More than 100 million tons of sugar are crystallized every year in refineries, from the liquid solution of raw sugar cane or beet. Even this spoon is a mass of silver crystals.

Liquid crystal display

Greatly enlarged photograph of crystals of vitamin C

Liquid crystal display
Liquid crystals are not truly crystalline. They flow like liquid but have properties, and molecules arranged, like crystals. Power rearranges molecules to reflect or absorb light.

Vital intake
These tablets have crystals of ascorbic acid, or vitamin C, in them—a white crystalline substance in plants, especially citrus fruits, tomatoes, and green vegetables. Vitamins are essential for health but cannot be produced by the body, and so are taken in through food or tablets.

Precious stones
Many people own jewelry with precious stones. This silver brooch contains diamonds, a blue sapphire, and a pearl.

Needlelike crystals in kettle fur

Kettle fur
Harmless minerals in tap water crystallize and coat the inside of your kettle when the water is boiled.

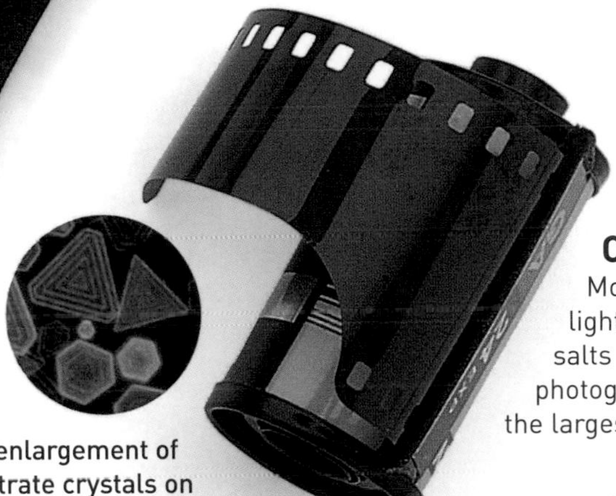

On film
Most photographic film uses light-sensitive crystals of silver salts to capture an image. The photographic industry is one of the largest users of silver.

Photo enlargement of silver nitrate crystals on a photographic film

Pressed for time
Quartz crystals control time (p. 31), and synthetic rubies (pp. 26–27) are used for watch bearings.

Ruby crystals

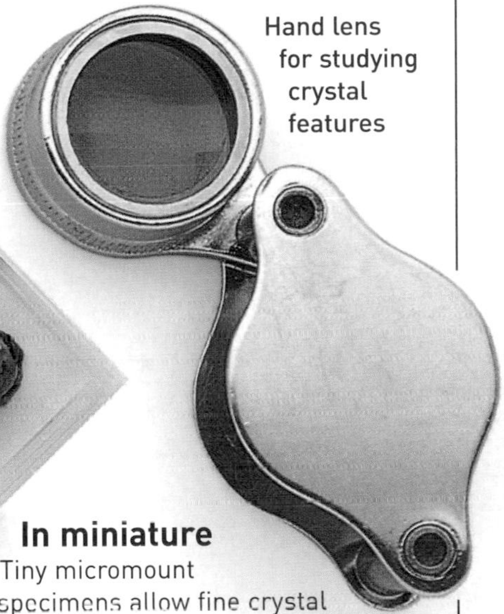

Hand lens for studying crystal features

Collecting
Crystals can be collected in the field, bought, or exchanged with friends and dealers. They are usually fragile and should be carefully stored with details of where they were found and, if possible, their host rock.

Wulfenite crystal

In miniature
Tiny micromount specimens allow fine crystal groups of rare and unusual minerals to be easily collected and stored.

Amethyst crystals

Cavity fillers
Fluids in basaltic lava flows often percolate through rocks and crystallize in available cavities.

Field work
Use a geological hammer and safety gear to collect in the field.

Did you know?

AMAZING FACTS

The Persians thought Earth sat on a giant sapphire and the skies were its reflection. Others thought the sky is a sapphire in which Earth was set.

Sapphire and diamond pendant

Sapphire-blue is a color associated with harmony, trust, and loyalty, which is why many women have sapphires in their engagement rings.

The name garnet comes from the Latin for pomegranate, a fruit with bright red, garnetlike seeds. Garnet colors vary from violet-red to burgundy.

Pomegranate

Diamonds can occur under the sea. People trawl for them in large, offshore ships, which pump gravel containing diamonds up to the surface.

Diamonds in kimberlite rock are mined on a huge scale. More than 27.5 tons (25 metric tons) of rock are blasted for every finished carat— 0.2 g (0.007 oz)—of diamond mined.

In medieval times, rich people wore diamonds to protect them from the plague. The ancient Greeks thought diamonds protected against poisons.

Moonstones are often set in silver to bring out their silvery sheen.

Moonstone necklace

People used to think a moonstone's opalescent luster waxed and waned like the Moon, so moonstones were worn by Moon worshipers.

Topaz crystals can be up to 3 ft (1 m) long and weigh hundreds of pounds. "Topaz" is thought to come from the Sanskrit word for *tapas*, meaning "fire."

The ancient Greeks believed amber was the hardened rays of a sunset and sacred to the Sun god Apollo. Amber can produce an electric charge when rubbed; "electricity" comes from the Greek word for amber, *elektron*.

Diamond dredging boats

Hawksbill turtle

Tortoiseshell carapace was widely used for hair ornaments

Tortoiseshell actually comes from turtles, from the shell of the rare (now protected) Hawksbill turtle. Most "tortoiseshell" in jewelry today is made of plastic.

Six-rayed star sapphires were once thought to protect against evil. The star's three crossing arms were meant to represent faith, hope, and destiny.

Star sapphire

The Egyptians believed lapiz lazuli's intense blue made it heavenly, using it on statues of their gods and in burial masks to protect them in the next life.

Cultivating pearls (making them grow by putting irritants into oysters) is faster than waiting for natural pearls to form, but it can still take up to four years.

QUESTIONS AND ANSWERS

Q How long have people been mining for gemstones?

A Jewelry containing gems has been found in burial sites dating back thousands of years. Some ancient Egyptian pieces, made of gold and set with gems, have also survived.

Q What are potato stones?

A Also known as thunder eggs, potato stones are geodes—hollow balls of rock with crystals inside. The crystals form when silica-rich liquids seep into bubbles of cooling lava.

Potato stones

Q Why are gemstones so precious?

A Because of their natural beauty, durability, rarity, and how they are cut and polished. There are 3,000 kinds of mineral, but only about 100 are gemstones, making them rare.

Q How are diamonds formed?

A Diamonds form at high pressure and temperatures deep inside Earth. Diamonds were first found 2,000 years ago in river gravel. Today, most diamonds are mined from kimberlite rock. Some of the main producers include Russia, Botswana, and Australia.

Q What are seed pearls?

A Pearls vary in size. The smallest are seed pearls. Pearls are not weighed in carats, but in grains. One grain—0.002 oz (0.05 g). Seed pearls weigh less than 0.25 of a grain.

Scarab beetle good-luck charm, found in Tutankhamun's tomb

Q Why were children often given coral jewelry in the past?

A To keep them healthy and safe; coral was thought to protect from evil.

Q Why are emeralds green?

A The green of emeralds comes from chromium and vanadium.

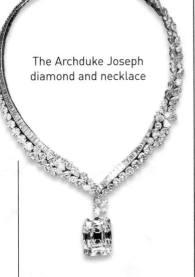

The Archduke Joseph diamond and necklace

Q Why are gemstones cut and polished?

A Cutting and polishing maximizes the amount of light gems reflect so they sparkle and shine.

Q Why are organic gems often carved rather than cut into facets?

A Organic gems, such as coral and pearl, are soft and often opaque, so light cannot shine through them, making it pointless to cut them into facets to increase their brilliance.

Q What is the connection between rubies and emery boards?

A Ruby is a variety of the mineral corundum, which is second in hardness to diamond. Emery is an impure form of corundum, and it has been used as an abrasive for thousands of years.

Cut ruby

Q Which famous ruby isn't really a ruby at all?

A Many crown jewels around the world contain red gemstones called spinels, which people mistook for rubies. The huge Black Prince's Ruby in the British Imperial State Crown is in fact a spinel.

Record Breakers

MOST VALUABLE GEMSTONE:
Diamonds, Earth's hardest mineral, are the most precious, famed for their fiery beauty.

BIGGEST DIAMOND:
The largest rough diamond ever mined was the Cullinan diamond, found in 1905 in South Africa, weighing 3,106 carats. It was cut into nine large and 96 smaller stones.

CUTTING MARATHON:
It took three polishers eight months to cut and polish the Cullinan 1 diamond, now set in the British Imperial Sceptre.

LARGEST RUBY:
The "King Ruby" in India is the largest ruby, weighing 48lb 6.43 oz (21,995 g).

BIGGEST BERYL CRYSTAL:
A beryl crystal from Madagascar was 40 tons (36 metric tons) and 59 ft (18 m) long.

Identifying gemstones

To the untutored eye, many gemstones look alike. They can be similar in color and cut. Here is a guide to the color and characteristics of some of the most popular gemstones.

Emerald lizard

Mixed-cut citrine with the orange tinge often seen in this gem

Citrine
Citrine is a yellow or golden form of quartz. Natural citrine (its name comes from the word "citrus") is pale yellow, but it is extremely rare.

Oval mixed-cut amethyst with a typical purplish violet color

Amethyst
Amethysts are purple quartz crystals, often with distinctive internal markings and a blue or reddish tinge.

Tiger's-eye, cut and polished to show up its stripes

Tiger's-eye
This chalcedony variety is a quartz-type made up of tiny fibers. It looks waxy and is black with yellow and brown stripes.

Typical reddish-orange polished stone from India

Carnelian
Also called cornelian, this is a translucent, reddish-orange or brown form of chalcedony.

Colorless, brilliant-cut diamond with black inclusions

Diamond
Made of pure carbon, diamond is very hard and shines brightly. The most popular variety is pure and colorless.

Cushion mixed-cut ruby in bright red

Ruby
The expensive, classic ruby is a rich red, but color varies from pink to brown. Rubies are hard, second to diamonds.

Pale blue Sri Lankan sapphire

Sapphire
The most valuable are a clear, deep blue, but can be yellow, green, pink, or colorless. It is a type of corundum.

Bluish green emerald with many tiny fissures and internal markings

Emerald
This beryl variety is a rich green. The finest are transparent and flawless. Most have flaws called a *jardin* (garden).

Octagonal step-cut aquamarine with a slight greenish tinge

Aquamarine
This beryl variety ranges from pale sea-green to dark blue. It can seem to change color from different angles.

An opal displaying flashes of green and blue

Opal
Known for its iridescence and flashes of color. Iridescent opal with a dark background is black opal. "Potch opal" is opaque, without any iridescence.

Salmon-pink colored topaz

Topaz
Topaz occurs in several different colors, ranging from deep golden yellow (known as sherry topaz) and pink to blue and green. Natural pink stones are extremely rare.

Watermelon tourmaline

Tourmaline
Tourmalines come in a range of colors, but they all have the same crystal structure.

Garnet
The most popular types of garnet for jewelry are pyrope, which is blood-red, and the deep red almandine.

Pyrope (garnet) cut as an oval

Octagonal mixed-cut peridot

Peridot
This olive or bottle-green colored gem has a waxy luster and strong double refraction.

A gray moonstone

Moonstone
Some are gray, yellow, pink, or green. Its name comes from its blue-white sheen.

Octagonal mixed-cut with a vitreous luster

Spinel
The most popular is ruby-red, but it can also be blue and yellow. Red spinels were once known as Balas rubies.

Cut yellow chrysoberyl

Chrysoberyl
Known for its golden color. One variety, alexandrite, appears to change from green to light red in artificial light.

Colorless zircon produced by heating a reddish-brown stone

Zircon
Pure zircon is colorless and resembles diamond, but it is more likely to be golden brown.

Translucent jadeite with black inclusions

Jade
Two different minerals, jadeite and nephrite, are known as jade. The finest jadeite is emerald green. Nephrite varies from cream to olive green.

Polished rock speckled with pyrite

Lapis lazuli
Prized for its intense dark blue, lapis lazuli is a rock made up of several minerals. Specks or streaks of pale pyrite and calcite are often visible.

Stone cut and polished as a cabochon

Turquoise
Turquoise is valued for its color, which varies from blue-green to bright blue. Opaque, it is usually cut and polished into rounded beads or cabochons.

ORGANIC GEMSTONES

Organic gems are derived from plants and animals. Amber, jet, coral, pearl, ivory, and shell are all organics. These materials are not stones and they are not as hard and durable as mineral gems. Instead of being cut into facets, they are usually polished or carved.

Carved jet with a finely wrought rose at the center

Jet
This fine-grained rock formed from fossilized wood. Black or very dark brown, it is opaque with a velvety luster. It is often faceted and polished.

Transparent golden brown beads that have been faceted

Amber
Amber forms from the hardened resin of trees. Transparent or translucent, it is usually a golden orange, but can also be a dark red. It sometimes contains insects and plants.

Amber necklace

Intricate red coral carving showing a monkey climbing a tree

Coral
Made of the remains of coral polyps, it can be pink, red, white, or blue.

A roughly spherical pearl suitable to be used as a bead

Pearl
Formed in shellfish, with an iridescent sheen, they vary from white and cream with a hint of pink to brown, or black.

Find out more

Natural history and geological museums usually have extensive rock and mineral displays and are invaluable sources of information on how crystals formed and what they look like in their natural state. Many also have good gemstone collections. There are many places where you can see how precious gems have been used in jewelry. Here are some suggestions for places to visit and websites to browse.

Crystals and gemstones
Most natural history and geological collections, like the ones found at the Natural History Museum in London, contain displays of cut gemstones and famous jewels. There are also crystals and gemstones in their natural state, often still embedded in their matrix (host) rock.

Where gems are found
Where gemstones are found depends on the geological conditions. This map shows the main locations of 12 of the most popular and highly prized gems. If you visit any of these areas, you may be able to tour mines or see samples of the gemstones in local galleries, museums, and stores.

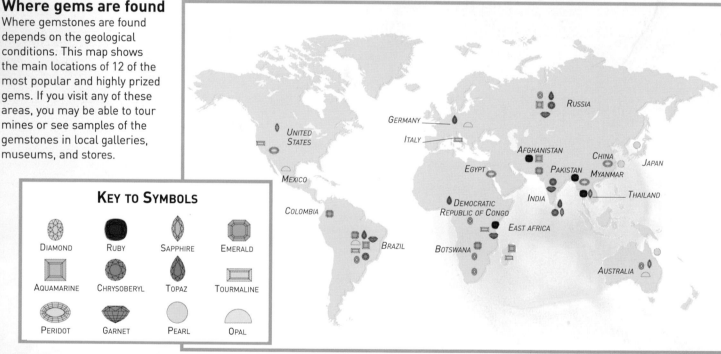

KEY TO SYMBOLS

DIAMOND   RUBY   SAPPHIRE   EMERALD

AQUAMARINE   CHRYSOBERYL   TOPAZ   TOURMALINE

PERIDOT   GARNET   PEARL   OPAL

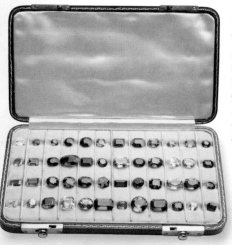

Gem collections
Why not start a gem collection of your own? Look for specimens on beaches, riverbanks, and hillsides. Clean your finds with water and arrange them in small cardboard trays. You can take them to a local museum for help with identification.

Cut gemstones that form part of the Matthews Collection in London, UK

USEFUL WEBSITES

- Learn about crystals and gems and find lots of resources and fun activities: **www.smithsonianeducation.org**
- See pictures of more than 1,000 different types of mineral: **www.webmineral.com**
- View the Smithsonian Gem and Mineral Collection: **www.gimizu.de/sgmcol**
- Find facts on more than 60 popular colored gemstones: **www.gemstone.org**

Jewels and jewelry

A museum of decorative arts will show you how gems have been set in jewelry over the ages, from historic pieces to modern jewelry in different styles. See if the museum has an ancient Egyptian section for early jewelry. If you travel abroad, visit local craft museums to see samples of ethnic jewelry.

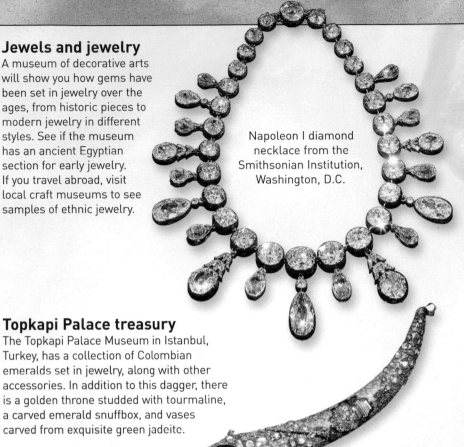

Napoleon I diamond necklace from the Smithsonian Institution, Washington, D.C.

Topkapi Palace treasury

The Topkapi Palace Museum in Istanbul, Turkey, has a collection of Colombian emeralds set in jewelry, along with other accessories. In addition to this dagger, there is a golden throne studded with tourmaline, a carved emerald snuffbox, and vases carved from exquisite green jadeite.

Dagger with emeralds set into the hilt

Crown Jewels

Examples of famous gems set in gold and silver are on display in the Crown Jewels of France, Britain, and Austria. The Louvre in Paris houses the coronation crowns of Napoleon and Louis XV, plus scepters, swords, and the Regent—one of the world's purest diamonds, worn by Louis XV at his coronation in 1722. The British Crown Jewels at the Tower of London include many jewels still used in state ceremonies today, such as the Imperial State Crown with the famous Black Prince's Ruby.

Charlemagne (742–814), king of the Franks

Gold set with precious jewels

Crown of Empress Eugénie on display at the Louvre, Paris, France

Golden scepter set with gemstones, made for Charles V in 1380

At the Tower of London Education Center in London, UK, schoolchildren can try on replicas of the Crown Jewels and royal cloaks, as well as armor.

Glossary

ALLOCHROMATIC Meaning "other-colored," it describes colorless gems that are colored by impurities.

ALLUVIAL DEPOSITS Weathered rock fragments that have been carried along in rivers and streams and deposited.

AMORPHOUS Without a regular internal atomic structure or external shape.

ASTERISM The star effect seen in some gems, such as rubies and sapphires, when they are cut into cabochons.

BIREFRINGENCE (DR) Double refraction, a crystal property in which light passing through is split into two rays.

Brilliant-cut diamond

BRILLIANT CUT The most popular cut for diamonds and many other stones. The standard brilliant has 57 facets, or 58 if the gem is cut with a flat face at the base.

CABOCHON A type of cut in which a gemstone is cut into a round or oval with a plain, domed upper surface.

Star ruby cut into a cabochon

CARAT The standard measure of weight for gemstones. One carat equals 0.2 g (0.007 oz).

CHATOYANCY The tiger's-eye effect of some stones when cut into cabochons.

CLEAVAGE The way in which a crystal splits apart along certain well-defined planes according to its internal structure.

COMPOSITION The fixed or well-defined chemical makeup of a mineral.

COMPOUND Two or more elements joined together chemicallt that can only be separated by heat or great pressure.

CORE The area of iron and nickel at the center of the Earth.

CRUST The thin outermost layer of the Earth.

CRYSTAL A naturally occurring solid with a regular internal structure and smooth faces.

CRYSTALLINE Having a crystal structure.

CUT The way a gem is cut into a number of flat faces called facets, or rounded and polished.

Calcite crystal

DENDRITES Fernlike growths of crystals that line rock cracks and joints.

DICHROIC A term that is used to describe a gem that appears to be two different colors when viewed from different directions.

Dendrites of the mineral pyrolusite

DIFFRACTION The splitting of white light into its constituent colors.

DOUBLET A composite stone made of two pieces cemented or glued together.

DURABILITY The capacity to last for a long time without wearing out.

EROSION The wearing away of land and rocks by a moving medium, such as ice.

FACET One flat surface of a cut gemstone.

FACETING Cutting and polishing gems into flat surfaces.

FIRE A term used for dispersed light. A gem with strong fire is unusually bright.

Fluorescent crystal

FLUORESCENCE Colored light that radiates from a mineral when it is exposed to invisible ultraviolet light.

GEMSTONE Mineral or organic material prized for its beauty, durability, and rarity.

GEODE A rock cavity lined with crystals that grow toward the center.

GIRDLE The widest part around the middle of a cut stone, where the top half (the crown) and the bottom half (the pavilion) meet.

HABIT The shape in which a crystal naturally occurs.

IDIOCHROMATIC Describes minerals whose color is part of their chemical composition.

INCLUSIONS Material (usually a mineral) trapped within another mineral.

Idiochromatic sulfur

INTERGROWN When two or more minerals grow together and interlock.

IRIDESCENCE A rainbowlike play of colors on the surface of a mineral.

LAPIDARY A skilled cutter of gemstones to obtain the best optical effect.

Iridescent hematite crystals

LAVA Magma from within the Earth that erupts to the surface from volcanoes.

LODESTONE A piece of magnetite, a naturally occurring magnetic iron oxide.

LUSTER The way a mineral shines, affected by how light reflects off the surface of the mineral.

MAGMA Molten rock deep below the Earth's surface.

MANTLE The layer between the core and crust of the Earth.

MASSIVE A term used to describe minerals that have no particular shape.

MATRIX A term for the main body of a rock.

METAMORPHOSIS Recrystallization in a solid rock, leading to a change in mineral composition and texture, usually caused by high heat.

Magma

MICROCRYSTALLINE A mineral structure where crystals are too small to be seen with the naked eye.

MINERAL A naturally occurring inorganic solid with regular characteristics.

MIXED CUT A gemstone cut in which the facets above and below the girdle follow different styles, usually a brilliant cut above and a step cut below.

MOHS' SCALE Devised by Austrian mineralogist Friedrich Mohs, the scale measures mineral hardness according to what a mineral can scratch.

NACRE Tiny platelets of calcium carbonate that create the sheen on pearls and some sea shells as they reflect light.

Nacre inside shell

OPALESCENCE Milky blue form of iridescence.

OPAQUE Does not let light pass through.

ORGANIC GEM A gem made by, or derived from, one or more living organisms.

PEGMATITE Igneous rocks containing very large crystals, formed from the very last water-rich magma to crystallize.

PENDELOQUE CUT Lozenge-shaped cut often used for flawed gems.

PHANTOMS Regular inclusions within a crystal, such as parallel growth layers.

PIEZOELECTRICITY A property of quartz crystals. Pressure on a crystal creates positive and negative charges.

PLEOCHROIC Describes a gemstone that looks as if it is two or more different colors when viewed from different directions.

PRISMATIC Describes a "pencil-like" crystal, with elongated crystals.

PROPERTY A characteristic of a mineral, crystal, or gemstone, such as its color.

REFRACTIVE INDEX (RI) A measure of how light rays slow down and bend as they enter a gemstone.

RESIN A sticky substance from plants.

RHOMB A shape a bit like a lopsided cube.

RIVER GRAVELS Deposits of minerals that have been broken away from their host rock and washed downstream.

Selenite

ROCK A combination of mineral particles; some contain multiple minerals, some only one. Rocks may be inorganic, chemical, or biological in origin.

ROUGH The natural state of a rock or crystal.

SCHILLER Sheen or iridescence.

SPECIFIC GRAVITY (SG) A mineral property that compares its weight with the weight of an equal volume of water.

SPECTROSCOPE An instrument used to identify different gemstones. It reveals the bands of light that a gem absorbs.

Coral, an organic gem

STEP CUT A rectangular or square-shaped gemstone cut with several facets, parallel to the edges of the stone. It is generally used for colored stones.

STRIATION Parallel lines, grooves, or scratches in a mineral.

SYMMETRY, AXIS OF An imaginary straight line through a crystal. If the crystal were rotated about this line, the same pattern of faces would occur a number of times in a full turn.

SYNTHETIC GEMSTONE An artificial stone that has a chemical composition and properties similar to the natural gem from which it is copied.

Step-cut ruby

TABLE CUT A type of step cut with a square table facet and girdle and parallel square facets.

TRANSLUCENT Material that allows some light to pass through it.

TRANSPARENT Material that allows light to pass through it; it is see through.

TWINNED CRYSTALS Two crystals of the same mineral that are joined together at a common plane—the twin plane.

VEIN An infilled joint, fissure, or fault. Veins are often made of minerals.

VITREOUS A term used for the glasslike quality of some gemstones. It is used to describe a gem's luster.

Twinned calcite crystals

Index

Acknowledgments

Dorling Kindersley would like to thank: Peter Tandy at the Natural History Museum for his expert advice and help; Karl Shone for additional photography (pp. 28–29, 62–63); De Beers Industrial Diamond Division for the loan of diamond tools (p. 29); Gemmological Association of Great Britain for the gem certificate (p. 57); Keith Hammond for the loan of the beryl crystal (p. 21); Nancy Armstrong for the loan of the prospector's brooch (p. 41); Jane Parker for the index; Dr. Wendy Kirk for assisting with revisions; Claire Bowers, David Ekholm-Jalbum, Sunita Gahir, Joanne Little, Nigel Ritchie, Susan St Louis, Carey Scott, and Bulent Yusuf for the clipart; David Ball, Neville Graham, Rose Horridge, Joanne Little, and Sue Nicholson for the wallchart; BCP, Marianne Petrou, and Owen Peyton Jones for checking the digitized files.

For this edition, the publishers would also like to thank: Niki Foreman for text editing, and Carron Brown for proofreading.

The publisher would like to thank the following for their kind permission to reproduce their images:
a=above; b=bottom; c=center; f=far; l=left; r=right; t=top

Alamy Images: vario images GmbH & Co KG 28bl; **Peter Amacher:** 48cl; **Ancient Art and Architecture Collection:** 9cl; **Archives Pierre et Marie Curie:** 31bc; **Art Directors & TRIP:** 69cr; **Aspect Picture Library/Geoff Tompkinson:** 28br; **Dr. Peter Bancroft:** 45cr; **Bergakademie Freiberg:** 12cl, 19br; **Bibliotheca Ambrosiana, Milan:** 13cr; **Bibliotheque St. Die:** 53cl; **Bridgeman Art Library, London / New York:** Egyptian National Museum, Cairo, Egypt 65tc, 18tl, 52tr, 58bl; Bibliotheque Nationale, Paris: 42tr; **Paul Brierley:** 16cr; **F. Brisse, "La Symetrie Bidimensionnelle et le Canada," Smithsonian Institution, Washington DC:** 37tr, 39t, 42br, 69tr; **Canadian Mineralogist,** 19, 217–224 (1981): 13tc; **British Geological Survey:** 63br; **A. Bucher/ Fondation M.S.A.:** 30tl; **Gordon Bussey:** 62tl, / Bibl. Magazin, Paris: 60br; © **Christie's Images Ltd:** 27br, 64tl, 65cb;

Christie's, New York: 57cl; **Bruce Coleman/ Michael Freeman** 52c; **Lawrence H. Conklin:** 49bl; **Corbis:** 64b, 69br; **Crown copyright:** 46cr, 53tl, 58cr; **De Beers:** 29bl, 29tc, 34cr, 35br; **Dorling Kindersley/Eric Crichton:** 47tc; **DK Picture Library:** Natural History Museum 66c; e.t. archive: 41br; **Mary Evans Picture Library:** 7tr, 15tl, 23br, 24cl, 38/39c, 38bl, 46tr, 57br, 61tr, 61bl; **Fondation M.S.A.:** lltl; **Michael Freeman:** 25tc, 37c; **Grukker & Zn, Netherlands:** 28tr; **Robert Harding Picture Library:** 44tr, 51tl; **Harvaard Mineralogical Museum:** 20cl; **Harvey Caphin Alaemeda, New Mexico:** 50tr; **Ernst A. Heiniger:** 39br; **Michael Holford:** 7cl, 37br, 44cr, 50br; **Image Bank/Lynn M. Stone:** 33cr, /Lionel ASY-Schwart:** 54bl; **India Office:** 36tr, 56tr; **Kobal Collection:** 35cr; **Kodak Ltd:** 63c; **Kunsthistoriches Museum, Vienna. Photo: Courthault Institute of Art:** 40tr; **Lauros-Giraudon:** 34bl; **S. E. Little:** Octopus card Ltd 28clb; **Mansell Collection:** 15bl, 35cl, 45c, 54tr; **Moebius/Exhibition Bijoux Cailloux Fous, Strasbourg:** 10bc; **Museum national, d'Histoire Naturelle, Paris:** 48cr; **Museum of Manking:** 52bl; **National Gallery:** 50bl; **Natural History Museum:** 15tr, 19tr, 19c, 33br, 40bc, 51br, 68tl / Frank Greenaway FRPS: 11bl, 21bc, /P.Krishna, SS Jiang and A.R. Land: 21tc, /Harry Taylor ABIPP 31br; **National Portrait Gallery, London:**

16c, 43tr; **Northern Island Tourist Board:** 22bl; **Perham's of West Paris, Maine:** 23tr; **Phototake, NYC/Yoav Levy:** 30cr; **Katrina Raphaell:** 31cr; **Réunion Des Musées Nationaux Agence Photographique:** Musée de Louvre 69bc, 69bl; **Ann Ronan Picture Library:** 27tc, 27cr, 55tc; **Royal Geographical Society:** 36bl, 39tc, 56bl; **S. Australian Dept of Mines and Energy/B.Sowry:** 41tc; **Science Photo Library:** 9tr, 14bl, /Dr. Jeremy Burgess: 6tr, 62c, 63tr, /ESA/PLI:8tl, / John Howard: 43cr, /Peter Menzel: 25c, /NASA: 26c, /David Parker: 9br, /Soames Summerhays: 8bl; **Brian Stevenson & Co:** 25bl, 59tc; **Stockphotos:** 20br; **R. Symes:** 20tr; **Uffizi, Florence. Photo: Giraudon:** 32cl; **Victoria and Albert Museum:** 51cr, 55bl; **Werner Forman Archive:** 61cl; **Peter Woloszynski:** 49cr; **Zefa/ Leidmann:**32tr, /Luneski: 60cl.

All other images © Dorling Kindersley.
For further information see:
www.dkimages.com